"I've known Erik since he was a child and saw firsthand how he dealt with a severe stuttering issue, and today I hear him as he leads others with a clear strong voice in so many arenas of life. Erik is a man of character and competency, which makes for an authentic leader. I believe in his message and you will be blessed as you read his book. His wisdom and warmth will inspire you to be your best!"

—**Dr. Dwight Ike Reighard,**
author and pastor of Piedmont Church, Marietta, GA

"After a string of successful (and some less successful) entrepreneurial ventures, I found myself in the founder and CEO position of a company that went from zero to $1 billion in sales within five years. I had so many questions and there were so many things I didn't know and wasn't prepared. Enter Erik Weir. Erik's wisdom, experience, counsel, and connections have been instrumental in helping me not only manage but grow these resources and find ways to use this financial blessing to serve the Lord and help other people. I'm so glad he's written a book to bring the unique financial insight I've come to depend on to the rest of the world!"

—**Chad Price,**
founder and CEO, Mako Medical Laboratories

"This book is a great reflection of who Erik Weir is on a daily basis. It is articulate, informed, and entertaining. When we were looking for a partner to expand Topgolf into several foreign countries, we needed someone who could share the vision and passion that others were cautious to embrace. Erik brought courage and optimism to our partnership, and millions of guests will have more joyful lives because of what we were able to do together. I am giving this book to my own children!"

—**Dolf Berle,**
former CEO, Topgolf Entertainment,
CEO of Lindblad Expeditions

"I'm blessed to have gotten to know Erik Weir over the past few years as I've transitioned from the NFL to a college coaching career. He's as much a teacher as he is an investor, teaching me a lot about real estate investing and how to build wealth that lasts."

—C.J. Spiller,
former NFL running back,
running backs coach, Clemson University

"Erik Weir is one of the most accomplished business people and financial instructors I know. He has a pure focus on living life to the fullest, maximizing all of his God-given potential, and leaving a legacy that fuels the next generation into their God-given destiny. He is a prolific instructor of CEOs in the areas of stewardship, fiscal leadership, and investment strategies. *Who's Eating Your Pie?* is sure to please and advance those who read with progress in mind."

—Hasker Hudgens, Jr.,
senior pastor of The Equipping Church,
Greenville, SC, Author of *I Am Evangelism*

"As a business partner with Erik for almost eight years, I can tell you that Erik and his business practices are 'the real deal.' Many business partnerships end badly. Erik and I not only had a successful run, but we continue to do work together to this day after we sold our company. Most importantly, I call him 'friend.'"

—Bill Reeves,
CEO, Educational Media Foundation,
KLOVE/Air1/AccessMore/WTA

"I've known Erik for many years, and he's always been looking ahead, finding new opportunities, and exploring the what-ifs? of the financial world. This new book explains some of his most practical money tips into a very digestible way."

—Jay Ward,
creative director of franchise at Pixar Animation Studios

"You could spend twenty years working, negotiating, winning, losing, and doing deals to figure out how to build wealth . . . or you could learn it all in a day or two just by reading this book. Erik's worked with my grandfather and my father, and now he's working with me, teaching me how to leverage the opportunities I have today as a young entrepreneur for long-term wealth building. I'm so glad to have met him as I'm just starting out!"

—**Cassidy Thompson,**
social media influencer

"Erik Weir and I met years ago when we attended the same church. We became awesome friends. Erik impresses me with his humble nature and his knowledge of the financial world. He's a powerful resource and he is my go-to guy on anything related to finance. I would endorse him with my life."

—**Levon Kirkland,**
former American football player,
member of the South Carolina Athletic Hall of Fame

"Erik has been a friend and mentor to me for over ten years. The financial and business guidance he has given me over this time has forever changed the financial and career trajectory of my family. Erik has taught me not only how to make money but also how to manage it for building wealth and helping others."

—**Chad Patterson,**
CTO, The Doula Group

WHO'S EATING YOUR PIE?

ESSENTIAL FINANCIAL ADVICE THAT WILL TRANSFORM YOUR LIFE

ERIK WEIR

Forefront
BOOKS

Published by Forefront Books.

ISBN: 978-163763-055-6 (Print)
ISBN: 978-1-63763-056-3 (eBook)

Cover Design by Bruce Gore, Gore Studio, Inc.
Interior Design by Bill Kersey, KerseyGraphics

Dedication

To my parents, Brian and Dawn Weir, who refused to let me wallow in fear, embarrassment, and self-pity because of the stutter that nearly prevented me from saying my own name. You taught me how to pick myself up, dust myself off, get past any failure, and push through any obstacle. Those are the lessons that made me who I am today. Thank you.

To my brother Mark, who always encouraged me to chase my dreams and never give up.

To my wife, Stacey, who loves me as I am and encourages me to continually dream big and go for it. She listened to me read endless excerpts from this book and helped me make my points and topics clearer.

To Harrison, Matthew, Patrick, Wyatt, and George Weir. As my sons, you were my first audience. Over the years, you have been on hundreds of meetings and walked a lot of real estate deals with me when we traveled together as you were being homeschooled. After the meetings, we talked about what happened, and I learned much from each of you as I saw things from your perspectives. I tried out a lot of the concepts from this book on you all, so thanks for being good sports—especially when I literally took bites out of your dessert to make a memorable illustration! You all have been blessings to me and a reflection of my own life that has both given me encouragement and allowed me to see opportunities for my personal growth. I hope I have been as good of a father to you as you all have been sons to me.

To Malachi Grist, thanks for trying to help me dress using more color. I am continuing to work on it. Maybe someday I can even wear more colorful sneakers.

To my childhood pastor, Ike Reighard, who inspired a ten-year-old to love God, live with joy, forgive quickly, and live in gratitude. Thanks also for introducing me to Zig Ziglar, whom I enjoyed meeting in person and whose humble and practical teaching I've listened to countless times.

To my karate instructors over the years: Chuck Norris, Grand Master Jin Kim, Richard Tirschel, Keith Vitali, and Richard Burnette. You each inspired me in many ways and taught me discipline and how to respect others. The amazing Code of Ethics taught by Chuck Norris, Richard Tirschel, and Richard Burnette remain guiding principles in my life still today—especially number 8:

"I will always be as enthusiastic about the success of others as I am about my own!"

Contents

SECTION 2
PLANNING
FINANCIAL SUCCESS

SECTION 3
ACTIVATING
FINANCIAL SUCCESS

Preface

*U*nless you run in some pretty specific financial or investing circles, or unless you've attended some of my live trainings, you've probably never heard of me. That's okay. I never set out to be famous, even though I have several fairly well-known friends. I did, however, set out from a young age to be financially successful. From the age of five, when I opened my first lemonade stand in my parents' driveway, I had a passion for business. I was pretty good at it too. In high school I started and ran a yard care business that gave me an income rivaling a few of my friends' parents. All through college I operated my own karate studios and bought, repaired, and sold cars, giving me a six-figure income before I was twenty. After graduating, I went to work selling investments for one of the country's leading investing firms and started earning $1 million per year in income by age twenty-nine. And that was just the beginning.

But here's the thing: I'm not bragging. I'm nothing special. I didn't come from money. My family wasn't wealthy—in fact, there were times when we had to live with family members because we didn't have a home of our own. I'm not a tech genius. I don't have movie star good looks. I could barely even speak clearly for most of my life due to a terrible, trauma-induced stutter. Nobody stuck a silver spoon in my mouth or rolled out a red carpet for me. I didn't have anything handed to me. What I did have, though, was passion, drive, grit, and a sincere belief that I could accomplish *anything* I set my mind to. For my whole life I've been foolish enough to believe that I could do whatever I wanted. And that belief—coupled with the simple, reproducible strategies laid out in this book—has given me a richer, fuller life than I ever could have imagined.

You can do the same thing. Ten, twenty, or thirty years from now, you could write a bio that dwarfs my own accomplishments. You can do more and go further than your wildest expectations. But it won't happen by accident. Your financial life is and will always be a series of decisions that lead you from where you are to where you're going. Where exactly that is—up or down, good or bad, rich or poor—is up to you. And it starts by answering a simple question: "Who's eating your pie?"

So, let's talk about that.

SECTION 1

UNDERSTANDING FINANCIAL SUCCESS

CHAPTER 1

Permission to Dream

*N*o!
I heard the word *no* more than two hundred times. For the same project. COVID-19 shut the world down, and I was trying to raise money for an American entertainment concept in Germany that was totally unknown while everyone was hunkered down in their homes.

Banks. Private equity firms. Venture capitalists. Potential investors. Potential partners. It started to feel like everyone with deep pockets across two continents was lining up to turn me down. But I wouldn't stop. I couldn't stop. I knew I had a winner. I just had to convince everybody else—convince them that the world would return to normal and that people would venture outside once again.

Topgolf is one of America's fastest-growing sports entertainment companies. It's basically Chuck E. Cheese for grown-ups, a chain of fun, golf-themed venues with a restaurant, games, indoor club seating, and driving range with interactive targets. I was introduced to the concept a few years ago when my son and I were traveling through Florida. We had some time to kill, and I noticed this huge three-story complex that clearly had something to do with golf. I thought it was just a driving range, but when we went inside, I was blown away by what I saw. The place was packed with all kinds of people—groups of guys hanging out, families having fun, teenagers, twentysomethings, retired people. There was something for everyone, whether you enjoy golf or not. We spent a few hours there and left with the biggest smiles on our faces.

Several months later, my family asked me what I wanted to do for Father's Day. I said, "You know what? Let's all go to Topgolf for the day!" I checked online, and the closest one to my home in South Carolina is in Alpharetta, Georgia. My five sons and I hopped in the car, we made the two-and-a-half-hour drive, and we all had a fantastic Father's Day. My five-year-old loved taking big swings at the ball and jumped up and down with excitement when he actually made contact. My older boys competed for the longest, most accurate drives—all while stuffing their faces with pizza, wings, and bottomless sodas. I realized it was the first time we'd been somewhere where the whole family was having an equally good time. We weren't the only ones either. Looking around, I saw teenagers on dates, other families with young kids, older couples enjoying a meal, and first-time golfers laughing about how terrible they were at hitting a golf ball.

It was one of my all-time favorite days with my boys. As a father, I was thrilled to have something so high-end and fun to do with my family. As an entrepreneur, I thought, *Man, I just spent five hours total driving to and from this place, and we spent a few hundred bucks there like it was nothing. There's something to this business.*

So, when I later saw a Topgolf under construction in my own hometown, I got excited. I knew the guy who owned the property they were building on, and I asked him if he could set up a meeting for me and the owners of Topgolf. A few weeks later, I flew to Dallas with the friend who sold land for Topgolf's use, my CFO, and my lawyer. Topgolf's management team explained their expansion goals, and I got *really* excited. I said, "I want exclusive rights to finance every Topgolf location you build anywhere in the world!" They literally laughed at me.

"It costs between thirty and fifty million dollars to build *each* location," they said. "How much do you have right now, ready to go?"

"Not even one dollar," I said. They laughed again. "But I can get it. I've done it several times for other businesses, and I can do it for you."

"No offense," they said, "but why should we give you this opportunity?"

I didn't flinch. "Because it's the best thing for you and Topgolf."

That *really* got them rolling. They were laughing and pounding the table, and one turned to the other and said, "I really like this guy!"

As things settled a bit, I explained what I meant: exclusivity increases value. That's why diamonds are more valuable than rubies, even though rubies are far rarer than diamonds. Because one family controls the majority of all the diamond mines, they can release a limited number at a time, thereby creating artificial scarcity. By giving me exclusive rights to finance Topgolf locations, they'd be creating a similar scarcity, which would make the investment far more attractive and exclusive to anyone I ever pitch the investment to.

After an hour of back-and-forth, they agreed to give me a shot. They said my partners and I could buy the North Miami location they had just started constructing if we could come up with the money within sixty to ninety days—a goal my partners and I hit after making tons of calls. The concept is easy to explain if someone has ever been to a Topgolf but very difficult if they had not seen one, particularly if they are a golfer. It seemed that non-golfers understand the concept better than people who enjoy golf. In fact, we not only bought the North Miami location but we acquired a second location about a month later in Texas. Within twelve months, we either owned or were in the process of funding *five* Topgolf locations in the United States. I didn't write a personal check for them, of course. Rather, I did what I do best: presenting this opportunity to other investors and structuring deals that benefit all of us. I was thrilled with my new venture and the new partnerships I was making, but I was dying to take it global. I knew this business would be a hit in Europe, South America, and Asia. I just had to convince . . . well . . . everyone else.

My thing is finance and structure. It's not staffing, managing, or developing a concept. Topgolf awards exclusive right to territories around the world in a disciplined way. I wanted to have Asia, Europe, and the Middle East; however, they were awarding exclusive territories to people who were extremely experienced in the local markets, so I was out. I had to get in. What could I do to get into Europe, Asia, and South America?

As it turned out, the individuals who were awarded exclusive territories had never funded a Topgolf or explained the concept to bankers or individuals. I had to convince them that my team and I could be invaluable in helping accomplish their dream of developing Topgolfs in their part of the world. Having participated in five US locations, we had more experience than any other team in the world—but we had raised money only in the United States. Would it be different in Europe or Asia?

We traveled around the world, meeting Topgolf franchisees in their home markets. Talk about a group of impressive and intelligent people! Could we help them? Could we add value to these well-connected and brilliant individuals? That was our plan, to use our experience to help their dreams come true and structure a deal that worked for the franchisee and our investors. We finally got our chance in Germany. After flying to Germany a couple of times to meet the European master franchisees and spending days with them on two separate trips, we decided to work together and make the dream happen.

No one thought it would work. Overseas investors had never heard of Topgolf, and American investors were skeptical the business model would work outside the United States. Potential partners in Europe had a long list of concerns. First, this was at the height of the 2020 COVID-19 pandemic, so everyone was wary of investing in public entertainment venues. Second, they were worried that only golfers would be interested in Topgolf. Third, they couldn't get their heads around what *type* of person would come. Every time I pitched the idea to investors or banks, I heard a different concern. So, we began to catalog the concerns and write responses for each. After hundreds of Zoom calls and socially distanced meetings, I figured out my pitch.

"Look, do people enjoy beer in Germany? Do they enjoy spending time with friends? Going out to eat? Having fun? *That's* what Topgolf represents. Forget golf. Focus on people getting together with friends and family to have a great meal, drink, and have the most fun they've had in a while. Don't you think *that* is something Germans can get behind? Do you think that people who are confined now will want to be entertained *more* or *less* in the future? Do you think people will want to socialize more or less after being distant for a year? Do they eat at McDonald's, Starbucks, or Five Guys Burgers & Fries? The same questions were asked in the 1950s: Would Germans eat a McDonald's hamburger? Would Germans wear jeans and sneakers, eat pizza, watch a Hollywood film, or listen to American rock and roll? How would you have liked to be on the ground floor of one of these opportunities? Well, now's your chance. You can get in on the ground floor of a new business that is sweeping America. I can't guarantee it will work, but as Mark Twain would say, 'History never repeats itself, but it sure does rhyme.' McDonald's restaurants are bigger in Germany than they are in America. What if Topgolf is next in line?"

After a couple hundred rejections, a bank *finally* took a chance on my dream, and we broke ground on the first European location. As of this writing, my partners and I have over $300 million committed in Topgolf worldwide—and that's just *one* of my businesses.

All told, I own dozens of different businesses in various sectors ranging from film, real estate, marketable securities, and financial management and consulting for some of the wealthiest people in the country. But it's not because I'm a genius (I'm not). It's not because I was born into wealth (I wasn't). And it's not because I ripped off anyone, took advantage of people, or had some privilege that others don't. My success in business and in wealth-building comes down to just a few simple things: I work hard, I work smart, I dream big, I solve problems for other people, and I set big goals. If you do those things, and if you pair them with the finer points of personal finance and wealth-building that I'll unpack in this book, you can achieve everything I have . . . and much more. It all comes down to how well you grow—and protect—your pie.

THE PIE(S) OF LIFE

The title of this book, *Who's Eating Your Pie?*, comes from an analogy I've used with my children. My five boys were at least partially home-schooled, and I have loved being around to teach them and partici-pate in their education. When we first got started, I was surprised to learn that teaching little kids wasn't that much different from teaching my financial clients. Everybody needs a *hook*, some image to connect theoretical concepts to real-world application. For adults, that hook is usually money or some intellectual concept. If you can show someone how a principle impacts the cash in their pockets, they'll usually stick with you. Children are different. Little kids don't have the same intellectual and emotional connection to money that their parents have, so I've had to be a bit more creative when teaching my sons about taxes, interest rates, rates of return, social programs, education, and so on.

One evening after dinner, I was struggling to explain the concept of taxes to my oldest, who was maybe eight or nine at the time. We were sitting at the table just as he started his dessert—an awesome apple pie with ice cream. That's when inspiration struck.

I said, "Okay, forget money for a minute. You like apple pie, right?" He smiled and nodded as he grabbed his fork and got ready to dive in. "Look at that, the chunks of apple are peeking out at you through the perfect squares of the lattice crust on top. The ooey-gooey goodness is bubbling off the top and dripping down the sides of the pan. It's all for you. Are you excited?"

"Yes!" he squealed, ready to take a bite.

"Hold on a second," I said as I grabbed my fork. "How would you feel if I ate a big bite of your pie?" He looked at me in disbelief as, in one smooth motion, I carved off a giant piece of his pie and ice cream with my fork and stuffed it in my mouth.

"But Dad! That's my pie! It's *mine!*"

I replied, "Well, son, now you understand taxes. Me stealing your pie is like taxes or bad decisions stealing your money. Whether you like it or not, someone is *always* going to try to swipe some of what's yours, so you've got to be ready for it." He nodded his head, then pushed my hands away as I dramatically went in for a second bite.

My son didn't have a job at nine years old, but trust me, he understood taxes from then on. That teaching tool worked so well, in fact, that I started using the pie analogy with my clients to help them understand the dangers they face with their money. But I didn't stop with taxes. As I thought about it, I realized we have many different people, organizations, motivations, emotions, mistakes, bad judgment calls, and relationships that are always trying to steal a slice of our pie. I also realized that we each have several different pies in our lives. We have a money pie. We have a health and fitness pie. We have a relationship pie. We have a marriage and family pie. We have a career pie. Basically, you can imagine *any* important area of your life as a pie—and picture any number of people and things who are trying steal it.

Sometimes the thieves are external, meaning they come from outside yourself. You might have a crummy boss who's always nipping at your career pie. You could have an angry ex-spouse who's trying to gobble up your money pie. Maybe you're dating an overly needy person who's claimed too much of your relationship or emotional pie. Whatever you care about, whatever pie you're focused on, I bet something or someone is trying to grab a slice.

I could write a book about a dozen different pies of life, but I want to keep this book laser focused on the money pie. How do we grow it into an even bigger, better pie? How do we keep everyone else's fingers out of it? Should we give part of the pie to other people? Is it okay to enjoy it for ourselves? Is it even *moral* to want to grow our money pie by building wealth? If so, what's the best way to go about it? How do real estate and stocks work? How do I build wealth as an employee? How do I build wealth as an entrepreneur or business owner? How do I build wealth as an influencer or an entertainer? So many questions, and each one has the potential to add to our financial pie—or gobble it up.

I've helped some of the wealthiest people in the country answer these questions, from multi-Grammy-winning music artists to CEOs of some of America's biggest companies to world-renowned professional athletes. Now, I want to do the same for you. I want to give you the same advice and guidance I've given to millionaires and billionaires, and we'll start with the same question I often ask them.

WHAT IS "RICH" AND WHY DO WE WANT IT?

I've found that everybody wants to be "rich," but almost no one stops to consider what it really *means* to be "rich" or why they even *want* to be "rich." Think about it: when you hear the word *rich*, what image comes to mind? A big house with a McLaren parked in front? Fancy clothes? Exotic vacations? The ability to buy whatever you want whenever you want it? Those things may sound nice (and granted, they are), but simply amassing a pile of *stuff* isn't the point of this book. Trust me on this: if you're driven by a need for more and more *stuff*, you have a hole inside you will never fill. No amount of stuff will make you feel successful. No one purchase will be *the thing* that brings contentment to your life. If all you want when you're broke is money, all you'll want when you're rich is *more* money. There will never be enough for you. Money, while solving some problems, often brings with it new problems previously not imagined. It's been said that money is a great tool but a poor master. The more money I've made, the truer that statement has become.

I grew up with parents who loved each other and loved me and my big brother. They both worked and we had nice things, but we weren't especially wealthy. We were middle class, and my parents experienced financial ups and downs. The ups were great. During the downs, we didn't have a home of our own and had to stay with family members. I slept on a relative's family room sofa for months. It seemed like fun at the time though. I didn't realize we were experiencing an unemployment issue until twenty years later. After that, my parents turned things around financially. But were we *rich*? I think we were, in a sense. It was safe and stable, and I lived in a loving home. Even though I had to sleep on the sofa for a while, we never had to stress about where our next meal would come from. My parents taught me to look for and chase after opportunities to improve myself. They taught me how to work. All those things made me the man I am today.

My family background, especially contrasted with my financial success in my adult life, has taught me that "rich" isn't a dollar amount; it's a *perception of relative comfort and security*. Each word of that definition is important, so let's break it down.

The Perception of Wealth

When I say "rich" is a *perception* of relative comfort and security, I mean there's a difference between *being* financially wealthy and *feeling* wealthy. A big part of wealth-building that most people discount is the *incredible feeling of peace* that comes when you no longer have to deal with the anxiety of being broke. At this point in my life, there is almost nothing I couldn't buy if I wanted to. In fact, as I write this, I am buying a fractional interest in a jet with friends. Yes, it's used. And yes, I'm buying it with partners to minimize cost. But hey . . . I am buying a freaking *jet*! When you step out of a jet, no one knows if it's new, used, leased, or fractionally owned. But I didn't buy it for appearances; I bought it because owning a jet (even with other people) will make me more money than it cost me. How? Because having access to this jet frees up more of the one asset I can't get any more of: time. A jet is a time machine. It allows you to get more done than you ever could without it. If having this jet gets me to just one meeting that I couldn't attend without it, I could do a deal that could pay for a *fleet* of jets. It's not about luxury; it's about opportunity.

I can't tell you how freeing it feels to be able to do that, to become more efficient, take people with me on meetings, and save time in security lines at major airports. The business we discuss on the plane ride often yields results that pay for the trip ten times over. There's something about being in a private jet that opens your mind to dream a little bigger and seems to have the same impact on the other passengers.

Now, buying a jet probably isn't among your immediate priorities. But what *would* make you feel rich? Maybe it's putting $1,000 in the bank for the first time in your life. Maybe it's having six months' worth of expenses in a savings account just for emergencies. Maybe it's being able to transition from two incomes to one so you or your spouse can be home with your kids when they're young. Maybe it's being able to buy your dream car. Whatever it is, I want you to identify *that thing* that would make you feel like the king of the world. Then I want you to write it down. Over time and as our wealth increases, it can be easy to forget those initial goals we set early in our financial journeys. Don't. Don't forget where you are *right now*. Don't forget what would make you feel rich today. Don't let your pursuit of more success in the future steal your chance to experience the joy of feeling rich today.

Wealth Is Relative

Have you ever heard the expression, "One man's trash is another man's treasure"? Well, I'd take it a step further and say, "One man's *poor* is another man's *rich*." If you grew up dirt-poor and living on food stamps, simply being able to walk into a grocery store with $250 to fill your cart with a week's worth of groceries would make you feel super rich. If you grew up with a fully stocked kitchen and never had to worry about money, that same $250 grocery budget could feel extremely limiting—even *poor*. What changed? How can the exact same scenario cause two different people to react in opposite ways?

It's because even though the *money* is the same, the *people* are different. Each person has different needs, wants, hopes, dreams, personalities, priorities, lifestyles, and backgrounds, and all these things (and more) play into how we understand wealth. Like I've said, "rich" isn't a dollar amount. Most of the time, being rich isn't about how much money you *have*; it's about how much money you *need*. Some people need a $400,000 income to feel rich. Others can feel just as rich on $40,000. One person would be scared to death to retire with "only" $500,000 in her retirement account, while another person would be jumping for joy. That's because wealth is *relative*—it *relates* to your specific situation.

This may not be what you expect to hear in a book on wealth-building, but the *relative* nature of wealth is a critical piece of your financial pie. People who miss this end up spending their entire lives working eighty hours a week in jobs they hate because they're focused only on what they're *making*. But what is that income *costing* them? They're miserable all day, every day, and no amount of money can pull someone out of that kind of emotional nosedive. This is why it's so important to set personalized financial goals, something we'll talk about in-depth later in this book. For now, though, I want you to focus on what wealth means to you specifically, in your life, with your unique set of circumstances. That way, you can be sure you're always working toward *your* wealth goals—and not someone else's.

Wealth, Comfort, and Security

Of all the wealthy people I've known over the years, I've never known anyone who has pursued wealth *for the sake of* wealth. Rich people know that wealth isn't about the money; it's about what that money allows them to do. Sure, there are plenty of people who get wrapped up in all the toys and trappings of money, but I've found most people are primarily concerned with providing their families with a safe, comfortable lifestyle. Whatever amount of money enables them to do that feels "rich" to them.

For example, I know a couple in their thirties who have four kids ranging from thirteen to five years old. He works as a graphic designer making around $50,000, and she stays home and home-schools the kids. The six of them live in a three bedroom house they rent, and they have only one car, which he drives to work, leaving the rest of the family stuck in the house all day, every day. To make matters worse, their landlord recently told them he was selling the house they live in, and he gave them thirty days to find a new place— in the middle of a housing boom when home prices and rents have skyrocketed and availability has plummeted.

What do you think "rich" would mean to this family? Though happy, they aren't *comfortable*. They'd love to buy their own home, the older kids are sick of sharing a bedroom, and they desperately need a second car. They don't need $5 million in the bank to feel rich. They'd feel plenty wealthy if they simply had a larger, modest home of their own with two older used cars in the driveway. All these young parents want for their family is to provide a safe, stable place for their kids to grow up, food on the table, clothes on their backs, and a second car to drive around. But these things have felt just out of reach from the day their first child was born.

Perhaps you can relate. You may be struggling as you read this book. Maybe you're a single mom, and "rich" would just mean the ability to pay your bills and get some sleep. Maybe you've recently lost your job, and "rich" would just mean having a steady paycheck again. Maybe you're facing retirement, and "rich" would just mean enough money every month to pay your bills without you having to move in with your adult children. Isn't that what we all want—just a little comfort and security?

When you're struggling to provide the essentials for your family, you'll never feel rich. But when you cover these bases and still have a little money stashed away for the occasional splurge, you can feel like a Rockefeller.

Sharing Your Pie

In 2017, I had the privilege of traveling to South Sudan to do some Christian mission work at one of the largest refugee villages operated by Samaritan's Purse. I saw poverty there that most people wouldn't believe could exist in the twenty-first century—whole families surviving on a one-gallon jug of oil and a bag of rice per month. But I saw something else in that village: *joy*. I saw children scream with joy when I kicked a new soccer ball to them. I saw their entire faces light up over something as simple as a stick of gum. That trip was a sobering lesson that happiness and joy are a choice, and it's a choice anyone can make regardless of the size of their bank account. It was also an unforgettable reminder that our wealth—no matter how much or how little we have—can be used to bring life-changing blessings to other people.

Giving is a priority for nearly all the wealthy people I know. There's a common stereotype of wealthy people acting like Scrooge McDuck, pinching every penny and diving into a pool of their own money. That doesn't line up with my experience at all. Instead, the wealthiest people I know are usually the most generous people I know. They view their wealth as a responsibility and as a resource to be shared with their churches, communities, charities, and fellow man. The more they make, the more they give.

The great speaker and author Zig Ziglar once said, "You can have everything in life you want, if you will just help other people get what they want." Don't miss that: the secret to *having* more is *giving* more. I believe that's not only a financial principle, it's also a spiritual principle. No, I'm not advocating some kind of prosperity gospel or a give-to-get mentality, but the truth is something happens in our hearts when we give. It causes us to take our eyes off ourselves and to see the world through someone else's eyes. If "rich" really is *a perception of relative comfort and security*, we must learn to get outside our own experience and understand what wealth means to other people. You could change someone's life with a simple gift. Take the family I mentioned. Imagine they lived next door to you, and you were about to replace your minivan. What if, instead of selling your old van for a few thousand dollars, you simply gave it to your neighbors, no strings attached? Can you even imagine what that would do for them?

And think about what that would do for *you*. You'd have the unmatched joy and excitement of knowing you made a huge impact on someone's life, and it really didn't cost you anything at all. They'd feel rich having a second car, and you'd feel rich for being in a position to donate one. Giving away money or stuff also increases your gratitude for what you have. Seeing someone receive a gift like that makes it nearly impossible for you to take what you have for granted.

GROWING THE PIE 1 PERCENT AT A TIME

Now that we have a better baseline understanding of what it means to be rich, let's talk about the concept of *building* wealth. We fall into ruts where we think our *pie* (whether we're talking about our health, finances, career, relationships, emotional health, etc.) is fixed. That is, we believe all we have now is all we'll *ever* have. But that's not true. No matter what pie we're talking about, you have the ability to *grow* it, to make it bigger. That's what wealth building is all about, and that's what we're going to talk about throughout this book.

I've been studying martial arts for about forty years, and I even taught karate for several years as a side hustle while in college. In all that time, I've never seen someone advance from no training to black belt in one day. Karate takes time, patience, and a lot of practice to master. No one would disagree with that when it comes to martial arts, so why do we often act like this isn't true in every other area of life? I've had countless conversations with people who were just looking for *the inside secret*, the hidden key to unlock a financial fortune overnight. Maybe you're reading this book because you're looking for a shortcut too. If so, I've got bad news: there is no shortcut to financial health and happiness. There *is* a path toward wealth and security, and it isn't too difficult to navigate, but it's a process—one that can be mastered over time.

The key to wealth building isn't unlocking some secret bit of knowledge. Rather, the key is making incremental improvements day after day in a progressive, continual march toward success. Oftentimes, when I'm speaking to a group of people, I'll ask, "Can you make a 1 percent change today? Can you simply make a tiny positive tweak to how you're doing things?" No one has ever said no. That's great, because there is more power in a daily 1 percent change than you've ever imagined.

For example, if I'm talking to someone who is grossly overweight and has tried and failed to get in shape for years, I'll say something like, "Can you eat 1 percent fewer calories tomorrow than you did today? If you had 4,000 calories today, do you think you could cut it down to 3,960 calories tomorrow?" Of course, they could. "Then, could you make another 1 percent change the next day, cutting your calories down from 3,960 to 3,920? Then another 1 percent change the next day, going from 3,920 to 3,880?" One percent is easy. Most people can make a 1 percent change and never even notice. But as you keep pushing yourself 1 percent further each day, you start making real progress you never expected.

In the same way, I might say, "Okay, you didn't do any push-ups today. Do you think you could do *one* push-up tomorrow? Then *one more* push-up the next day? Then *one more* push-up the day after that?" Again, pushing the envelope in such a tiny way isn't scary. It feels manageable to anyone, no matter how out of shape they are. However, after only ten days, this person will have cut their calories 10 percent, and they'll be doing more push-ups than they've ever done in their life. More importantly, they'll have taken more positive steps for their health than they've taken in years. This is how you effectively *grow your pie*.

When I walk an audience through the 1 percent challenge, I'll ask, "What if you made daily 1 percent changes in other areas of your life, like your health, relationships, education, career, emotional health, and thought patterns? Do you think you could make a tiny 1 percent change in those areas too?" No one doubts they can; they only doubt how much difference 1 percent makes—until I combine the 1 percent challenge with the Rule of 72.

In finance, the Rule of 72 is a simple way to determine how long it will take an investment to double in value. If you divide 72 by an investment's interest rate, or its rate of return, you see how long it takes to double that investment. For this discussion, our investment is our pie (whichever *pie* you want to focus on), and the interest rate is 1 percent. Dividing 72 by 1 leaves you with . . . 72! That means you can literally double your productivity in any area in just 72 days by making tiny, 1 percent improvements.

But it doesn't stop there. If you are two times more productive after 72 days, what happens 72 days after that? At 144 days, you're *four times* more productive than you are today because you're doubling the double. Another 72 days later, you're *eight times* more productive than you are today. Go one more round, and you are *sixteen times* more productive than you are today. And this is less than ten months after you started! Who doesn't want to be sixteen times more productive in a key area ten months from now? You can do it, and you can do it by making only a 1 percent positive change every day. And as you become more productive, focused, and disciplined on that key area, it begins to grow—maybe slowly at first, but that slow start leads to exponential growth before you know it. That kind of steady progress is what took me from a starting salary of $22,000 at age twenty-two to over a $1 million per year within five years, and it's what has taken many of my clients to even greater levels of success!

The bottom line is that you aren't limited to the small pie you're served. You can grow it however big you want—*if* you follow the strategies I'll unpack in the chapters ahead. Be warned though: money is never *just* about money. Your wealth will grow as *you* grow. There's a reason RadioShack and Blockbuster went out of business and BlackBerry's business suffered: they couldn't keep up with the changing demands of the day. They thought the skills of yesterday would take them into tomorrow, and they were wrong. The same is true for you. If you are the same person ten years from now that you are today, you'll be in the same financial shape by then—or worse.

If you want to grow your *wealth* exponentially, you'll need to grow *yourself* exponentially. That's why we're going to talk about *you* at least as much as we talk about your money throughout this book.

SERVING YOUR FINANCIAL PIE

I've said that everyone has many different pies in their life—emotional, relational, professional, and so on. There are books to be written on all of them! But *this* book is laser focused on your *financial* pie. This is my chance to share with you my thirty-plus years of experience in the financial game and all the incredible lessons I've *learned from* and *taught to* some of America's wealthiest men and women. I've assembled basic maxims that can help *anyone* go from rags to riches, from lack to plenty, from debt to excess. And it all comes down to figuring out who is eating your pie—*and how to stop them.*

I like the pie metaphor because it's simple enough for a child to understand, but I also like that the pie is *round.* It reminds me of the "Wheel of Life" concept that the great Zig Ziglar used to teach. Ziglar taught his crowds to think of their lives as a wagon wheel with seven "spokes" coming out of the center. Those spokes represented your career, financial, spiritual, physical, intellectual, family, and social lives. He explained that we must strive for harmony across all seven areas. Otherwise, we'll end up with a flat spot on our wheel, and that guarantees we'll have a bumpy ride. When all seven spokes are at equal length, well maintained, and balanced, however, the wheel can keep rolling on and on forever, taking us anywhere we want to go.

The financial pie works much the same way. If you neglect any one of the areas we'll discuss, you'll end up with a frustrating, unsatisfying experience. Some bites will be delicious, other bites will be bitter and spoiled, and still other bites will be bland and neutral. I don't want bland pie. If I'm ponying up to the table with my mom's apple pie, I want to absolutely savor every delectable morsel.

I've been fortunate enough to spend a lot of time with millionaires and billionaires over the past thirty years. Most of these men and women—heck, nearly *all* of them—have been self-made, meaning they went from practically nothing to millions or even billions all on their own. Some of them were tech geniuses who struck it rich overnight. Some, like me, set a goal to hit millionaire status before they turned thirty and made it happen. And some took the long road, slowly and steadily building wealth and building businesses over the course of years and decades as they made good decisions over the long haul and ultimately reaped the rewards of their time, patience, and discipline. There's no *one right way* to do it. No secrets. No shortcuts. It's all about making smart moves over time as you both *defend* and *grow* your financial pie.

That's what this book is all about. It's a collection of the most important money concepts I've picked up over the years. This is what I'd tell you if you were one of my clients. It's what I'm teaching my five sons about how money works. And it's how a stuttering kid who could barely say his own name became one of the most successful and sought-after financial advisors in the country.

Whether you realize it or not, *you already have a financial pie.* Now, it's time to learn what to do with it.

Grab a fork, and let's dig in.

CHAPTER 2

The Psychology
of Success

I've learned firsthand that most people's biggest limiting factor
when it comes to their money isn't their education, background,
stature, gender, race, orientation, occupation, or tax rate. Their
biggest limiting factor—*your* biggest limiting factor—is limiting
thoughts. It's the little voice in the back of your head that says, *I can't.
I shouldn't. I won't. I'll fall. I'll fail. I'm not smart enough. I'm not strong
enough. I'm not successful enough. I'm not [fill in the blank] enough.*

Sound familiar?

The adage is true—we really are our own worst enemies. Most
of us spend our whole lives backing down, not from actual adversity,
but from the limiting forces in our own minds. Sure, we blame other
people. We point fingers. We whine about "the system." We spout
nonsense about how the little man can't get ahead. But those are
just the excuses we tell ourselves because we don't want to face the
simple truth: *it's our fault.* Wherever you are in life, good or bad, it's

because that's where *you* have brought *yourself*. I can't help you with your money until you deal with that reality. If you want to take your life and your finances to the next level, you've got to reframe your thinking around what it means to be successful. It's time for a paradigm shift, and I'm the guy to bring it to you. I'm more concerned with your *success* than your *feelings*. And that means we've got to first tear down the mental and emotional walls you've constructed. Walls that are standing between where you are now and where you want to be. The same walls I've had to smash myself my entire life. The same walls that I still face every day!

Grab a pair of steel-toed boots because I'm about to stomp on your toes. But first, let me tell you my qualifications.

MY NOT-SO-SECRET SUPERPOWER

"H-h-h-h-h-hello. M-m-my n-name is E-e-e-e-rik W-w-w-weir. H-how-how c-c-can I e-earn y-y-y-your b-b-business?"

Doesn't sound like the greatest cold-calling sales pitch, does it? Believe it or not, though, that's the opening line that took me from a $22,000 starting salary at age twenty-two to a $1-million-per-year income by age twenty-nine in 1996. (That's about $1.7 million in 2021 dollars assuming about 2.2 percent inflation.[1]) It's not a traditional success journey, but it was the hand I was dealt—a stutter I had to learn to live with for most of my life.

That journey started in 1972. I was five years old when my family of four—Mom, Dad, my older brother, and me—was involved in a terrible car accident. I remember every horrifying detail. The sound of the collision. The car being jolted around and my little body being thrown against my brother in the back seat in the days before anyone cared about seat belts. And then . . . the eerily calm stop. Everything went from wildly out of control to strangely still in a matter of seconds. Believe it or not, it's that stillness that freaked me out more than anything.

Police officers arrived on the scene very quickly, even before we managed to get out of the car. I remember the officer's stern-yet-compassionate voice as he said, "You folks need to stay in the car for now. We'll let you know when you can get out." But that car was the *last* place I wanted to be. I was convinced it was going to explode. It was all I could think about. My heart started racing. I couldn't catch my breath. My mind and body were in full-blown panic mode.

I wanted to do as I was told—*stay in the car*—but I could not for the life of me understand why my mother and the police officer were so cavalier about two little kids who were about to die in an earth-shaking fireball in the middle of the road as rubberneckers drove by seemingly unconcerned. Five-year-old Erik was freaking out.

My mom turned back to me and said, "Erik, honey, calm down. We can't get out yet."

"But we're going to explode! We have to get out of the car right now!"

"We're not going to explode, Erik," she said.

I was unconvinced. I remember sitting in that back seat for what felt like hours, certain we were all seconds away from blowing up. The red and blue lights of the police car kept flashing across my face. The sirens wailed every time another patrol car, fire truck, or ambulance pulled up. The lady who hit my mom was put on a stretcher and wheeled right past my window into an ambulance. It was all too much for me. By the time the police gave us permission to leave the car, my mind was shot. The car may not have blown up, but my brain sure did.

Later that night, after the police reports had been filed and the car towed away, the four of us were sitting around our kitchen table trying to relax and enjoy dinner. That's when my parents noticed something in me had changed.

"C-c-c-can I h-h-ave m-more po-po-po-potat-t-toes?"

My parents looked at me with real concern in their eyes. They said, "Erik, is something wrong? Are you okay?" Well, I wasn't injured, but I certainly wasn't *OK*. I had no problem thinking; I knew what I *wanted* to say but something was wrong. It felt like the words got stuck to the roof of my mouth like a giant spoonful of peanut butter. I couldn't push them out. It was terrifying—not just to me but to my parents as well. Though none of us was physically injured, I had sustained horrendous emotional trauma that manifested in a terrible stutter. And sadly, the resulting speech impediment wasn't temporary. It is something that has shaped my life every day since that scared little boy was finally allowed to get out of the wrecked family car.

I'm sure when something like this happens today, parents and doctors take a much more sympathetic approach in treating the child. Rather than focusing only on the speech issue, doctors and counselors would most likely identify the *real* cause of the problem—the emotional trauma of the car accident. Back in the early seventies, though, emotional issues weren't taken as seriously. Today, five-year-old me would probably have a team of counselors and therapists helping me unpack the trauma of that one terrible afternoon. Back then, I just had a speech therapist sit me down and say, "Look, nothing is going to come easy for you in life. You're going to have to fight to speak, fight to communicate in order to be successful. Or . . . you can give up and become a huge failure in life. Is that what you want? Because that's the choice you have, young man. Fight to win or give up and fail. There's really nothing in between for you."

Tough love or tough luck?

My parents took this advice to heart, though, because they could see the potential I had even at that young age. All the teachers, counselors, and speech therapists agreed that I had a quick mind, but it was trapped behind what they saw as a physical problem—my stutter. The only way around it, they argued, was *practice.* They encouraged my parents to be intentional about giving me opportunities to speak to people. Mom and Dad were warned that, if they didn't *push* me to talk to people, I'd probably withdraw, become something of a recluse, and learn to avoid people for the rest of my life. That's probably true on some level. I was already having issues at school. My classmates loved to make fun of me and started calling me Stutters almost immediately. It didn't help that my father changed jobs once or twice a year as he advanced in his career. I was rarely in the same city for more than six months until I was twelve years old, which meant I changed schools a couple of times during the average school year. New school, new classmates, new bullying. Kids love to pick on the new guy—especially if he can barely say his own name.

Not long after the accident, in the face of nonstop insults and mocking, I was proud to be named "Prince of the Fall Carnival" at school for selling the most cookies in a fundraiser. Finally, a bright spot for a little guy who desperately needed some encouragement. That bright spot, though, soon turned into a spotlight—one that brought laser focus to my speech impediment. I was brought up on stage to receive my award, but the surprise and stage fright made my stutter ten times worse. They put the microphone in my face and told me to introduce myself, but I couldn't even say my own name. The teacher cried for me as I stepped offstage and sank back into my seat. The overwhelming feeling of shame mixed with anger at the kids pointing and laughing at me was awful. My mom tried to put on a happy face and brag on my accomplishments, but I was really down and found it hard to celebrate. I cried myself to sleep that night. It was the first of hundreds of nights I'd cry myself to sleep as a child.

Turning Lemons into Lemonade . . . Literally

That same year, my parents helped me set up a lemonade stand at the end of our driveway. The speech therapists had been clear that I needed to be *pushed* into social situations where I had to talk to people, and they thought a friendly neighborhood lemonade stand would be a great way to get started. Even at five, it was clear that I had an entrepreneurial mind. My folks figured the lemonade stand would give me a financial incentive to get out in the world and talk to people. They were right.

I still didn't want to talk though. Not only was it embarrassing but it took *forever* to spit the words out when I tried to say something. To make things worse, the letters *E, W,* and *F* are especially hard to say when you stutter—tough times when your name is *Erik Weir* and you priced your lemonade at *fifty* cents. And what are the two questions every well-meaning grown-up wants to ask a kid selling lemonade? "What's your name?" and "How much?"

Mom helped me make the lemonade, set up the table, and prepare a stack of paper cups, and I was open for business. I spray-painted a sign that read, "Lemonade 50 Cents." And, unlike what you might see these days, I was happy to find that our neighbors actually stopped at my little stand. Everyone was friendly and supportive of the new business on the block.

When they asked how much it cost, I pointed to the sign, hoping to avoid having to speak. No dice. Every single customer repeated their question, practically demanding that I speak or engage in the sale. I stuttered as I spit out, "F-f-f-fifty c-c-cents."

I learned an important lesson that morning which has been crucial in my business life for the past fifty years: as bad as a stutter might have been at school, it can be great for business. I discovered that most people are (somewhat) kind at heart, and they want to see the underdog win. When someone sees another person—especially a little kid—struggling to overcome some adversity, they naturally cheer them on. That's why some of the most popular books and movies of all time feature the triumph of an underdog. When it came to my lemonade stand, cheering me on meant giving me tips. Hardly anyone paid me only fifty cents. Rather, people were giving me dollar bills. A few even handed me a five. Every time I sold a cup of lemonade, I would get two, five, or ten times the price in the form of a tip.

When my dad got home from work that night, he asked me how it went. "G-g-g-great!" I said. "I m-made ei-ei-eighty dollars!" Eighty dollars is a lot of money for a five-year-old *today*; in 1972, it was a fortune. If you're curious, $80 in 1975 is about $400 in 2021 dollars.

"Are you serious?" my father asked. "Erik, I'm not sure *I* made eighty dollars today!"

I was hooked. The next morning my parents were at work, so my brother and I were home alone. I went into the kitchen, made my lemonade, got the table and glasses, and set up shop for day two.

Once again, all the neighbors stopped, and I was forced to struggle through what seemed like a hundred conversations as my customers bought lemonade. And, like the previous day, I sold every drop—and made a pile of cash.

Later that evening, my mother was setting the table for dinner when she noticed something odd in the cabinet. After double-checking the cabinets, sink, and dishwasher, she looked at me puzzled and with a furrowed brow. "Erik, do you know where the glasses are?"

I exclaimed, "Yes! I s-s-sold them all!" That's right. Without her there to help that afternoon, I'd skipped the paper cups and sold our entire collection of glassware—for fifty cents each.

So, on my second day in business, I learned yet another important lesson: the painful reality of *cost of goods sold*. I had to replace my family's glassware out of my hard-earned cash, which killed my zeal for lemonade sales (and educated me about the cost of glassware). That was it for the lemonade stand, but it was just the beginning of my professional life and my journey of leveraging my greatest weakness—my stutter—into one of my greatest advantages.

Now I want to be clear about something: I'm not saying *pity* is the secret to success. I don't think my neighbors were taking pity on me by buying my lemonade any more than I think any of my billionaire financial clients or business partners have taken pity on me in the fifty years since. However, my stutter has been a part of me for most of my life, even though it finally started getting better in my thirties once I accepted it as a part of me—a part I could even be grateful for—and not as some kind of foreign plague sent only to embarrass me.

Rather than letting it tear me down and derail my plans for success, I had to figure out how to leverage my stutter into a strength by taking an honest look at who I was, what I was working with, and what I could do with it. Most importantly, I had to make a decision: would I let my stutter stop me or would I figure out a way to *use* it—along with every other strength and weakness in my arsenal—to move ahead and push through walls?

The choice was up to me.

SUCCESS IS A DECISION

Legendary CEO Jack Welch once said, "Face reality as it is, not as it was or as you wish it to be." That's some of the best advice you will ever hear. The appeal to "face reality as it is" is one of the simplest yet most difficult jobs we're called to perform. It requires us to lay down our masks, quit the excuses, and take a good, hard look in the mirror. That's something few people are prepared to do. Yet the happiest, most fulfilled, and most successful people I know are the ones who've *had it* with trying to look like something they're not and who have not only accepted but embraced who they truly are. They have decided to be successful, no matter what it takes, no matter how big a hill they have to climb, and no matter what obstacles they have to overcome.

But there's a problem: choosing success requires us to stop lying to ourselves and other people. It feels so gross to admit, but it seems like we're lying about *everything* these days, doesn't it? I know people who are embarrassed to be who they are—embarrassed to speak their mind, dress differently, have a different point of view, or even act like everything might not be someone else's fault. It's always been a challenge, but our modern "cancel culture" has made it ten times more difficult for people to be their authentic selves. Whether it's politics, religion, health, appearance, career, or money, most people are spending way too much time and energy lying to themselves and others about who they are and how well (or poorly) they're doing. They're so invested in looking perfect that they're basically living a lie, leading a double life that is inconsistent with their values and what they know to be true. Bottom line: they're lying to themselves and everyone else, and they're just hoping they can keep the lie going a little longer. Chances are, they won't. The longer you lie to yourself, the harder it is to maintain the illusion that everything is okay.

Beyond lying about who we are and how well we're doing, we also struggle with lying about where we're going and what we plan to achieve. A friend of mine is horribly overweight, borderline obese. For years, he's told me that he's going to lose weight. He'll talk about how much he's researched different diets and how excited he is to try new workouts. The problem? He's never actually done any of it. He likes thinking about it and talking about it, but that's where he stops. It's enough for him to think about being healthier and fitter. It makes him happy to think about how much better his life will be *someday*. But I know someday isn't coming.

After years of listening to this, I just cracked one day. He said something about how he's going to lose a hundred pounds, and I blurted out, "No, you're not. You're just not. You *could*, but you *won't*. You've been talking about this for years. If you were serious about this, you would have done it by now. You don't want to lose weight; you just like thinking you do. What you really want is to dream about losing weight without having to change any of your diet or exercise behaviors. It makes you happy to talk about weight loss like it's the reality, but the reality is that you enjoy talking about weight loss more than you'd enjoy putting in the work to actually do it."

I know that sounds harsh, but I wasn't really beating him up. I was trying to give him permission to be happy being overweight. It's his life. He can be as big as he wants. We like to tell ourselves that we're supposed to be this or that, but the reality is that no one really cares. Nobody cares what our goals are. No one else cares what size we are, how much money we make, what we do for a living, whether we go to college, what clothes we wear, or any of the other things we agonize over day after day. I think my friend would be a lot happier if he just made the decision to be a big guy. Just own it. Instead of lying to himself and everyone else about how he's going to lose weight, he could just say, "Yeah, I'm overweight. I like to eat. I don't like to exercise. I like going out to dinner with friends, trying new foods, and drinking beer. I love bread and cake and cookies and cinnamon rolls. I know there's a health impact, and I can keep an eye on that side of things, but I'm tired of pretending like I'm *supposed* to be skinny. I'm not. I'm me, I'm big, and I'm happy."

In doing this, he'd be making his own decision about what he wants to do. Is it the best decision? Who's to say? But it would be his decision. He could willfully decide to be a happy overweight guy and then get on with his life. He could take all the time and energy he used to spend reading diet books and watching workout infomercials and put that into something he'll actually do. A few years from now, he might decide to lose weight and get healthy. Great! But again, that works only if it's his intentional decision that he's willing to back up with his actions.

As I write this chapter, my oldest son is working on a ranch in Idaho. He was struggling through some frustrating times in life and decided, "I hate what I'm doing, and I don't want to be here right now." So, he took a semester off school, headed West, and got a job doing something he enjoys. He's spending the spring riding horses and roping cows, and he's loving it. I'll admit that I, as his dad, was not thrilled at first when he took a semester off. I am, however, incredibly proud of him for taking an active role in his own life, and now I am fully onboard and believe he made the right decision for himself. He saw some things that weren't working and were making him miserable, and he decided to make a change. He chose what he wanted to do, and then he actually did it. He may or may not go back to school later, but what's more important is that he's already demonstrated a life skill too many people never grasp: choosing his own version of success.

Successful people don't go with the flow; they steer the ship. When it comes to your money, there will be a million people giving you a million different pieces of advice about what to do, what to invest in, what kind of investments are best, how much you need, and so on. You can do anything from stuffing cash in a mattress to betting on red with one spin of the roulette wheel in Vegas. There's no *one way* to build wealth, and there's no set amount that makes you "wealthy." It's all up to you. You get to choose how much you want. You get to choose how quickly to get there. You get to choose how much risk you're comfortable with and which investments line up with your priorities, goals, and values.

The bottom line is that you get to choose the size of your pie. And whatever you decide—or if you don't decide at all—you can't blame anyone else for what you get. It's your choice to make, and, for better or for worse, you're the only one responsible for how good or how bad the outcome is. And that's because . . .

IT'S YOUR FAULT

It's your fault.

That may be the most taboo phrase in the English language these days. In fact, if you're reading this in your early or midtwenties, it's possible you've never even heard someone say those words to you. Our world is increasingly against the notion of personal responsibility. Everyone from helicopter soccer moms to hand-holding college professors to our elected government leaders is telling young Americans that someone else is to blame for their problems, mistakes, and shortcomings. Can't pay your student loans? Clearly, the system is out to get you. Can't get a good job in your field? It must be a problem with capitalism. Got a speeding ticket? The cops are corrupt. Oh, woe is me.

No.

How about this: You can't get a job because you aren't a good, qualified candidate. You can't pay your student loans because you're too proud to wait tables. You got a speeding ticket because you drive too fast. I'll say it again: it's your fault.

Wherever you are personally, professionally, and financially, it's on you. It'd be nice to be able to blame someone else or, heck, blame the entire American capitalist system, but that's just passing the buck. The system isn't the problem; you are! There is one—and only one—thing every problem you have has in common: you. You are where you are today because of your decisions, period. But don't tune me out just yet. This is actually great news! This means you are the one with all the power. Not your boss, not your friends, not your competition, not your coworkers—*you*. And remember, you are the only one who can and should determine what success looks like for you. So if you're sitting there unhappy with what you've got, you know you need to make some changes. But if you are happy with it, you may not need to make any changes at all.

Say you've got a small financial pie. You're paying your bills, you have a place to live, you can afford to buy groceries, and you have a few bucks for entertainment every month. You aren't making huge strides forward, but you aren't going backward. You're just getting by. Some people may be in that situation and feel miserable. They may be frustrated beyond belief, spending all their time thinking about what they don't have and scheming how to grow their pie. Great! If that's you, you know you have some work to do. Clearly, you aren't happy with your financial situation and (hopefully) you're ready to take responsibility for improving things. It may be time for a new job, a lot of overtime, a roommate to split the bills with, or some other action or decision that will help generate more income to grow your pie. You're responsible for where you are, and you're responsible for kicking it up a notch.

However, someone else may be in that exact situation with those same circumstances and feel perfectly happy and content. She may feel no need to change a thing. She could enjoy her job, even if it pays a modest salary. She might love the freedom of a set work schedule with no overtime and having her nights and weekends free. She may value time more than money and be unwilling to trade her precious free time for a higher income. Of course, this person won't grow her financial pie as big as the person who actively wants to build more wealth, but who cares? She's happy. She's made a decision about what she values, and she's tailored her life around that. Does that make this person less successful than the one who works sixty hours a week to get ahead professionally? It depends on how you define success. The person who values more money would say no. But if you define success in terms of happiness, freedom, and general satisfaction, then this young lady is enjoying incredible levels of success. Why should she change anything? There is absolutely nothing wrong with wanting a small pie or a big pie. The point is, I just want you to make that choice. Don't settle for life's default options.

Now, let's say you've taken stock of where you are, and you truly aren't satisfied with your financial situation. You've chosen to go after a bigger pie. What do you do? I have some good news. First, the rest of this book is going to show you how to grow your financial pie by building wealth. That will include equal parts personal development and financial strategies, so buckle up. Second, I want you to understand that if you are the *problem* in your finances, then you're also the *solution*. The cavalry is not coming. No one is going to rush in to solve your problems for you. If you aren't happy where you are, you've got to make a change.

People sometimes act like all they need to do in a bad or unfulfilling situation is to hold on, stay the course, and wait for things to get better on their own. These are the people who, like my overweight friend, waste years talking about changing their lives *later*. Flash forward ten years, and most of the people are still exactly where they are today—unhappy and medicating themselves with wishful thinking. Why hasn't their situation improved? Because they haven't done anything to improve it. The second law of thermodynamics states that an object in motion tends to stay in motion unless acted upon by an outside force of greater or equal mass. If your life is going in one direction, it's going to keep going in that direction unless something or someone turns the wheel or hits the brakes. That "outside force" has to be you.

Failing to take responsibility for your own life and success leads directly to failure in all areas of life. You can count on it. If you take a passive approach to your life, you will not be successful. If you sit there and do nothing except think about what you *wish* you had, you'll never have it. You will fail. It's one of life's few guarantees.

But—and this is a huge *but*—the inverse is also true. Remember, you are both the problem *and* the solution. If failing to take responsibility for your life leads to failure, what do you think leads to success? That's right: Taking responsibility. Making an active change. Charting a new course. Setting your sights on where you want to go and being intentional about doing the things that will take you there. It won't happen overnight, it's not easy, and there will be days when you want to quit, but success happens on the way to your goal. You won't be successful when you get to the destination; you'll be successful the moment you start heading in that direction.

In his phenomenal radio presentation called "The Strangest Secret," famed motivational speaker Earl Nightingale defined success as "the progressive realization of a worthy ideal (or goal)." Notice he didn't say success is achieving a worthy ideal; it's the progressive realization of a worthy ideal. The phrase *progressive realization* is crucial. That means we're successful not just at the end of the journey but at every step of the way—as long as we're working toward the goal we've set for ourselves. If your goal is a bigger financial pie, you won't instantly have more money the moment you decide to shoot for it, but you will be more successful than you were the day before simply because you've taken a step toward your goal.

Nightingale says, "The human mind is one of the most powerful forces in the universe, and we each get the opportunity to steer and direct that force every day of our lives." I don't want to sound hokey or trite, but I firmly believe that if you can see it, feel it, and believe it, you can achieve it.

The trick may just be to get out of your own way. We'll talk about that next.

CHAPTER 3

The Pit of Self-Sabotage

No one will steal more of your financial pie than you will. That sounds strange, doesn't it? I mean, how can I steal from myself? Easy. We steal our own pie when we sabotage our own success. This is when we get in our own way by saying things like,

- I'm not smart enough.
- I am too young.
- My parents set me up to lose.
- The world is out to get me.
- I can't afford to make a change.
- The deck is stacked against me because of my race/gender/ physical disability.
- I can't win because of my stutter.

Any of these sound familiar? These are examples of limiting thoughts, and they will take a huge bite out of your wealth, mental health, and your wealth-building potential. The big problem is that these things don't just steal from the pie we already have, they actively *limit* us from growing our pie. It's a double whammy. Instead of getting more (like we should), we get less.

In the previous chapter, I beat you up over the issue of personal responsibility and tried to convince you that, good or bad, you are exactly where you've brought yourself. Now, I want to pull back a bit and try to explain why that so often leaves us so far short of our goal(s). Why exactly do we end up limiting our own success?

FAILURE IS EASY

The world expects you to fail.

You may even expect yourself to fail or, more commonly, hope for the best but expect the worst.

That's a harsh reality they don't teach you in school, but think about it: how much easier is it to fail than to succeed? Anybody can fail; it takes no effort. Plus, our system is chock-full of safety nets to catch people when they fall. Social services, Social Security, unemployment, food stamps, family services, Medicaid, and more are provided by the government. Ministries and nonprofits step in to provide basic housing assistance, food pantries, homeless shelters, job training, drug and alcohol rehabilitation services, and more. Believe it or not, our whole society is geared more toward encouraging our failures than celebrating our successes. I know that's a bold statement. The biggest complaint you're likely to hear is not that failure is common but that the successful are somehow gaming the system and not paying their fair share. The whole issue of welfare is a political hot potato and is, of course, much more complex than I'm making it out to be here. I just want to give you a new perspective on these things that you've heard about your whole life.

I'm not saying we should get rid of the programs and ministries designed to help people. We absolutely should be helping people who are struggling. I just want to call attention to the fact that the system makes it easy for people to fail and can even disincentivize people from striving to win.

Now, contrast that with how some people react to their own success. Those of us who actively strive to win can be surprised by what winning feels like. After working toward a goal for years, actually achieving it can feel strangely empty. Or, more often, it brings new pressures and problems we never expected. Why do you think so many young celebrities die or burn out so early? There's actually a cultural phenomenon called the "27 Club," which refers to the long list of popular actors, musicians, and artists who died at age twenty-seven. Jimi Hendrix, Janis Joplin, Jim Morrison, Kurt Cobain, and Amy Winehouse are all on the list. These and other creative superstars hit culture-shaping levels of success in their twenties. The outside world assumed they had it all, but they were plagued with isolation, self-doubt, imposter syndrome, depression, and addiction. Why? I believe it's because of the immense pressures and stress of success—a topic no one talks about for fear of seeming ungrateful or immature. Besides, no one wants to hear a rich, successful person complain about how tough their life is, right? Isn't that the very picture of privilege we hear about all the time on the news and social media?

So, let's see . . . the world expects us to fail and has a million programs ready to catch us when we fall. Our hearts are inclined to help people in their failures. We know how to comfort someone in their struggles, but we don't know how to support them in their success. We're intimidated by the success of others, especially those close to us. We're intimidated by our own success and even the *possibility* of our success. What on earth do you think that does to us over time?

It programs us for failure.

GETTING PAST "I CAN'T"

The two most damaging words to the pies of life—whether it's money, relationships, career, or anything else—are *I can't*. Nothing has ruined more lives, stolen more hope, prevented more joy, and raided more pie pans than telling yourself, *I can't [fill in the blank]*.

This little phrase is so destructive, in fact, that I outright forbade my children from ever saying it. Whenever they said something like, "I can't do math," I stopped them in their tracks and addressed their self-limiting thoughts immediately.

"No," I'd say. "Never ever ever say you *can't* do *anything*. Instead, say, '*I presently struggle with . . .*'" When you say *I can't*, you immediately limit your options and your success. When you say *I presently struggle with*, you are admitting a weakness ("struggle") but acknowledging the problem is only temporary ("presently").

For example, I'm currently taking a course on microeconomics at Harvard. I understand the basic concepts, but there are a ton of finer points and little details that I'm not familiar with. I don't understand it all right now, but that doesn't mean I can't understand it. It just means I presently don't understand it. But I can fix that by studying, doing my assignments, and putting the effort in. If I told myself on the first day of class that I can't do it, I'd have no reason to even try. If I tell myself I presently struggle with this, then that just encourages me to crack open the books and learn it. It makes me look forward to the day when I don't struggle with it. There is a world of difference between *I can't* and *I presently struggle*, and only one of those options will ever lead to success.

Focus on the Opportunity, Not the Limit

As I sit here writing this in late 2021, the COVID-19 vaccines have been in distribution for a while now. The coronavirus pandemic is still a top story on most news outlets, and the country is lining up to get their shots and move on with their lives. The past eighteen months have definitely been a strange time for America and the world. I know many people who have lost loved ones, money, jobs, investments, and entire businesses in the past year and a half. This virus and the subsequent lockdowns have shown us the limits of our income, health, and patience.

But if you come at it from a different perspective, it has shown us much more than our limits. In fact, it's shown many people more opportunity than they've ever had before—*if* you know where and how to look. Amazon and other online retailers have exploded. The personal computer industry—long in decline—had its first growth year in a decade. Mom-and-pop restaurants that were forced to close their dine-in service discovered even stronger profits in takeout and delivery sales. America's workforce as a whole was forced to get comfortable with working remotely, using previously out-of-touch technologies like Zoom and Slack to connect with their teams and get work done. Believe it or not, there is around $5 trillion sitting in money market accounts right now throughout the world. There is more cash available for spending and investment right now than there's ever been in the history of the world! Yes, many businesses have shuttered over the past year, and that is tragic. But let's not lose sight of the fact that many other businesses have not only survived but thrived during this whole ordeal. Why is that?

Even in a good year, if you were to ask the average person, "Can you start a business in the next year?" they'd almost certainly say no. If you stood beside them on a sidewalk looking at a big, beautiful home and asked, "Could you buy this house?" they'd likely say no. If you pointed to a brand-new Tesla Model S driving by and said, "Could you get one of those for yourself if you wanted one?" they'd probably say no. *I can't* is the typical person's default position, and that was true long before COVID hit the scene. As William Shakespeare wrote, "Our doubts are traitors and make us lose the good we oft might win by fearing to attempt."[2] The problem yesterday, today, and tomorrow isn't that we don't have opportunities; the problem is that we can't see the opportunities laying on the other side of our limits. We see the obstacle, the barrier, the boundary, the limit, and we think, *That's it. That's as far as I can go.*

But what if it's not?

The reason some people—from *Forbes* 500 CEOs to the average Joe—managed to thrive in the midst of a global pandemic and economic shutdown is that they have the ability to look *beyond* the supposed limits to see the massive opportunities most people never notice. Think about it. Elon Musk doesn't know how to build a car, and he isn't the world's leading battery scientist or physicist. However, he's built a company that is on the cutting edge of the automotive industry, battery technology, and even space travel! Steve Jobs wasn't a computer engineer, but he managed to create a company that literally changed how the world interacts with technology and communicates with each other. Kanye West didn't know a thing about event planning, concert promotion, publishing, or distribution, but he built himself into one of the most powerful names in the entertainment industry. What did these guys have that you don't? Intellect? Talent? Connections? Start-up capital? No! I'd bet the only thing that separates you from Elon Musk, Steve Jobs, and Kanye West is *vision*.

When all you can see are limits, your vision is impaired. Forget looking miles down the road and plotting a course to get where you want to go; you can't even see past the speed bump ten feet ahead of you. You might come up with the best business or product idea in the history of the world, but if you stop the first time someone tells you no, you will steal from your own future and rob the world of your revolutionary idea. Or worse, you'll drag your feet long enough for someone else to come up with the stroke of genius you've been sitting on. Then you'll be forced to watch someone else get rich on an idea you had first.

People with vision don't give up just because they don't personally have the know-how to bring their idea into the real world. They don't stop at the limit; they push through to the opportunity by partnering with other people to make it happen. I don't personally have $100 million sitting in my bank account, but I regularly structure $100 million business deals. The key is to connect your vision to someone else's ability or resources, creating a win-win scenario for both of you. Exactly how you do that is a bit past the scope of what I want to do here. My goal in this chapter is simply to show you that the limits stopping everyone else don't have to stop you!

Every now and then I'll take one of my five sons to a business meeting with me so they can experience these concepts in action. After witnessing one meeting, one of my boys said, "Dad, you just told those people that you could potentially turn a big profit for them by building this $50 million building. Where are you going to get the money to do that?"

I just laughed and said, "From them! Isn't that great?"

"But," he asked, "how are you going to build this? You're not a construction guy. You're a financial guy."

This was a huge opportunity for me to teach him to see beyond apparent limits. I said, "Imagine you had a magic wand that removed all limits from something big you wanted to do. If you had all the money, talent, time, technical experience, and resources in the world, could you do it?"

"Sure, I guess I could if I had all the money and resources and stuff."

"Great," I replied, "So here's the deal. You *do* have all the money and resources in the world. If you have a vision for something big and come up against a limit, your job is to connect with other people who have the money, knowledge, and resources you don't have and convince them to help you push past that obstacle. And in the process, you can give them opportunities to make money for themselves and participate in the success along with all the other people helping to advance the ball. That way, you personally keep pushing forward *and* you help other people push forward on their journey. The key is, you don't have to be the one who knows everything and does everything. You just have to be the one who comes up against an obstacle and says, 'Who or what do I need to help me push past this limit?'" It takes a team to accomplish great things, and it takes a great vision to motivate a team.

This way of thinking wasn't evident only in people trying to run businesses and survive during COVID; you can see this disregard for limit-based thinking in the very treatment of the virus itself. It is crazy to me that no one had even heard of COVID-19 prior to 2019, yet scientists have already developed multiple vaccines that have been through testing, trials, approvals, and now mass distribution. That's insane from a medical and historical perspective! Yet here we are. How did this happen? It's because someone took charge and said, "It's got to be done this year." Then, when the supposed experts told him it was impossible, he said, "I don't care if it's impossible. We're doing it anyway." And we did.

Everyone feels limited by something, whether it's education, intellect, race, gender, income, upbringing, or something else entirely. Whatever it is, we've got to see beyond the limit. We have to push through, wave our magic wand, and imagine those limits disappearing. Even if you don't know how to make your dream happen yet, I at least want you to start seeing the opportunity on the other side of the limitation. Once you catch a vision for the opportunity, you'll feel more of an inner drive to push through and grab it.

Redefining Failure

But what happens if you reach for the opportunity and still come up short? Does that mean you failed?

When I first approached the owners of Topgolf, I campaigned hard for the exclusive right to finance all their locations anywhere in the world. You'll remember that they laughed at me and said no. Instead of getting exclusive global rights, I "only" partnered with the individuals who got exclusive rights to all European locations and the chance to buy additional American locations. Was that a failure? No! I didn't get everything I wanted, but I got a heck of a lot more than I would have if I hadn't even shown up or if I had quit at the first objection. In that situation, I had three options.

First, I could have never set up a meeting with Topgolf. That would have been easy. The minute I had the idea about buying Topgolf locations, I could have given in to all the negative voices and limiting thoughts that filled my head. I could have believed the little voice that whispered, "What if this doesn't work? Where will you get the money? Why would you invest in an entertainment venue when people aren't even allowed to gather indoors without a mask?" I could have seen all the limits standing between me and the opportunity and stopped right there. Fortunately, I didn't do that. I pushed through the limits and prepared well for my meeting.

Second, I could have made my pitch, heard their laughter, and stopped when they said no. If I had done that, I could have gone back home telling myself, *Well, I did my best. It's not my fault they weren't interested.* This is where we comfort ourselves by blaming other people. If you understand that you are responsible for your own success, you already know this isn't a good option either.

Third, I could have made the pitch, heard their objections, and pushed past it. Instead of stopping when they said my plan wouldn't work, I could have pushed through by saying, "Okay, well what about *this*: Instead of exclusive worldwide rights, how about you give me exclusive rights in Europe or introduce me to the people you gave those exclusive rights to? You don't have any locations there yet anyway. You're expanding so fast in the United States that you probably don't have time to deal with the complexities of international business. I do or I can help the team you have selected structure and raise capital. I can help you own that market and champion Topgolf for you there. And I can still finance locations here in the United States as they become available."

Clearly, that's what I did, and it worked. By simply pushing a little further and refusing to quit, I turned their *no* into a huge— but slightly different—*yes*. Remember, money or opportunity is not finite. There are people who would love to own a Topgolf in Miami but who'd be terrified to own one in Germany and vice versa. One does not limit the other.

Where would you have stopped? My guess is that more than 90 percent of people would never have even made the pitch to the owners. That is so sad to me. I can't even fathom how many brilliant ideas have been allowed to fall to the ground and die simply because people are too scared, lazy, or intimidated to champion their own ideas. Maybe you've heard the phrase, "Ideas are a dime a dozen." That is so true because ideas are *everywhere*. Everyone you know, including you, has likely come up with at least ten different million-dollar ideas. But almost no one follows through. Why? Because they don't think they're qualified? Because they don't have the money, resources, or technical know-how? Because they don't value their own imagination and intellect? Every product, service, and business you know started with an idea from someone just like you. The only difference between you and that entrepreneur is that he or she took the next step, found the people they needed to work through the limitations, brought their idea to life, and championed it to others. They literally created something out of nothing. The whole process is a miracle! And the best part is that it's a miracle any one of us can perform!

We'll talk a lot about the mechanics of building wealth later in the book. For now, I just want you to believe that it is possible—and that it is possible for *you*.

THE POWER OF LONG-TERM PERSPECTIVE

In 1970, Harvard researcher Dr. Edward Banfield wrote a book called *The Unheavenly City* that presented his vast research into the area of personal financial success. He wanted to explain why some people achieve financial independence and wealth while so many others do not. Going into the study, Banfield had all the same assumptions and biases that we have today. He thought he'd discover the secret to financial success had something to do with background, family of origin, education, intelligence, or access to influential people. To his surprise, none of that was true—at least not to any significant degree. Instead, the overwhelmingly common attribute he discovered among the successful adults he interviewed was a particular way of thinking, which he called "long-term perspective." Summarizing Banfield's findings, personal development expert Brian Tracy writes,

> [Banfield] said that men and women who were the most successful in life and the most likely to move up economically were those who took the future in consideration with

every decision they made in the present. He found that the longer the period of time a person took into consideration, the more likely it was that he would achieve greatly during his career.[3]

Basically, Banfield discovered that the quickest way to make long-lasting, effective changes in your life is to change how you think. People who were intentional about planning ahead, fixing their minds on future goals, and being confident of the outcome were exponentially more likely to become successful—even if that success looked a little different than they originally thought. More than anything else, Banfield discovered, success is rooted in our thinking.

This is something automotive pioneer Henry Ford knew full well when he proclaimed, "Whether you think you can or you think you can't, you're right." For example, imagine a footrace between two track stars. Both are in similar physical shape. Both have clean, healthy diets and maintain a strict training regimen. Both prioritize proper sleep habits and arrive at the race well rested and ready to run. The only difference between these two as they step into the starting blocks is how they think. One believes she *will* win, and the other hopes she *can* win. Who do you think will cross the finish line first?

You'll most likely see the biggest difference in the last leg of the race. When their bodies are tired and the finish line is in sight, some people stop pushing themselves. They begin to release the tension that fueled their preparation. They feel a thrill that they've made it this far. In a sense, they give themselves permission to ease up just a little bit. And that's when they lose the race. The winner is the one who refuses to let up until the race is over. With everything else being equal, the race is won or lost in the mind.

Ever since I was a little kid, I've tried to be intentional about guarding my thoughts against the creeping specter of self-doubt. One of the best tools I've found to maintain my mental optimism and excitement is what I call a *victory book*. This is simply a journal or scrapbook that is dedicated to capturing your thoughts and feelings whenever you accomplish a goal you've set for yourself. When I achieve something I've been working toward, I always take time to celebrate the victory and commemorate the occasion by jotting it down in my victory book. Then, when I'm discouraged or facing failure, I can read back through all my old victories and find encouragement from all the successes I've experienced so far. I love looking back on previous challenges that seemed so impossible at the time yet turned into breakthrough victories that led me to higher levels of personal, professional, and financial success.

Even if you don't think you have any accomplishments to record yet, I encourage you to create your own victory book. Then, whenever you experience a big win—especially if it's the completion of a long-term goal—take five minutes to jot down your thoughts. I like to do it in paragraph form so I'll get the full impact of the experience when I read it back years later. For example, if you're trying to put $10,000 in the bank strictly for emergencies, you might celebrate the halfway point by writing,

> *May 15, 2021: With today's paycheck, I was able to get my savings account up to $5,000. I have never had this much money in the bank before! I never thought I could do it, but here I am, halfway to my $10,000 goal. It is so comforting to know I can handle a car repair or other emergency without completely freaking out about how to pay for it. I feel a sense of security I've never felt before!*

Today's victories become fuel for tomorrow's battles. Taking the time today to record your victories is one of the best gifts you can give "future you."

MAKE YOUR OWN LUCK

George Bernard Shaw wrote,

People are always blaming their circumstances for what they are. I don't believe in circumstances. The people who get on in this world are the people who get up and look for the circumstances they want and, if they can't find them, make them.[4]

That's the attitude I live by. I've talked to so many people who blame their poor decisions, faults, failures, and shortcomings on bad luck. Or other people. Or timing. Or the economy. Or the government. Or their boss. Or their customers. Or their spouse. Or anything else that could save them from having to take responsibility for their *whole* life, the wins and the losses. But luck doesn't exist. Luck is just another way of talking about opportunities and how well or how poorly we take advantage of them.

From the time I opened my first lemonade stand at five years old, I've found that the harder and smarter I work, the luckier I am. When I get lazy or don't pay attention to what I'm doing, "bad luck" has a way of sneaking up on me. Isn't that strange? It's almost like I'm making *my own* luck. Well, guess what? I am. And, more importantly, so are you. When you come up against a limitation and put your brain and back into the hard work of pushing through it, you create a better outcome for yourself. You may not get the thing you want in that moment, but you are building strength, resolve, and discipline that will empower you to push through even greater obstacles next time. That is a tremendous reward in and of itself. I'll be the first to admit that I've failed *a lot* throughout my life and career. I've won a lot too. And every one of those wins and losses has led me to where I am today.

Where are your wins and losses taking you? Are you heading there on purpose or are you being led through your own life by fear and uncertainty? We'll deal with that issue next.

CHAPTER 4

Where Do You Want to Go? (And Where Are You Right Now?)

*M*y role as a financial advisor and wealth manager basically comes down to helping my client answer two key questions:

1. Where do you want to end up?
2. Where are you right now?

That's it. It's not that complicated, but it's always amazing to me how few people are actually able to answer these two questions honestly.

Whenever I ask people these questions, I can practically *see* the pressure build up in their faces. Their view of where they want to end up is usually something crazy, something a million miles from where they are right now. There's nothing wrong with that; I'm an ambitious guy myself. In fact, we'll spend an entire chapter later discussing how and why to set big goals. The real problem lies with the second question. Asking someone where they are in their financial/aspirational journey *right now* triggers something deeply emotional for most people. It's like their hopes, dreams, fears, and ambitions all get stuck in their throat at the same time, choking the life out of them.

Why?

In this chapter, I'm going to teach you a tool for assessing where you want to go and where you're starting from. But first, I want to address what I think is the biggest emotional blocker that prevents people from answering these two questions: guilt. Asking someone about their long-term goals and then immediately asking them where they are right now on their way toward those goals bring up a wave of guilt and disappointment for most people.

If that's where you are right now, take a breath. Nobody's judging you. Nobody even knows where you are in your journey. Even if they knew, they wouldn't care. This is 100 percent a matter for you (and your spouse, if you're married) to figure out on your own. Besides, facing the fact that you're not where you want to be or where you think you need to be isn't necessarily a bad thing—if you take the right lesson from the insight. All you're doing is figuring out where you are on the map. You look back on where you started, you look ahead toward where you want to go, and you figure out where you are right now. It's like keeping an eye on your GPS on a road trip. Are you almost there? Halfway there? Just pulling out of your driveway? Are you lost in your own neighborhood? Whatever the answer is, you *need* that answer in order to get on the right track toward your destination.

Good or bad, embarrassing or not, you can't go anywhere (on purpose) without first facing your current position. That's the difference between a modern GPS and the old, giant Rand McNally paper maps my dad used to unfold and lay over the hood of his car when we got lost on vacation. A paper map can show you all the roads and destinations, but it doesn't know where you are. Without that crucial piece of information, you aren't going anywhere. The journey is a lot easier when you're clear on both point A *and* point B.

Besides, the journey is so much more enjoyable when you are honest and intentional about what's standing between you and where you want to go. I like to think about what a great artist like Renoir, Picasso, or Michelangelo thought on day one of a project, when they were staring at a blank canvas or a slab of stone. Do you think Michelangelo was sad, guilty, or depressed that his sculpture wasn't finished yet? Do you think he mourned over the fact that the rough piece of marble didn't look anything like the vision he saw in his head? No! Instead, he took joy as he looked at that rock because he could see the beauty and potential within it. He knew on the first day what it would look like on the last day. His job, then, was to simply chip away everything that got in the way of the masterpiece he knew was trapped inside the stone. That's what I want you to do. I want you to be honest about what you're looking at today, get clear on what the finished product can and will look like, and then start chipping away at everything standing in your way.

GET YOUR BEARINGS
WITH A SWOT ANALYSIS

Whenever I consider jumping into a new business deal or making a big investment, I always run through what's called a SWOT analysis. SWOT is a simple acrostic that stands for *strengths*, *weaknesses*, *opportunities*, and *threats*. Businesses have used this tool for many years to ensure they have a full top-down view of themselves and the other factors at play when they're facing a big decision. I've been doing this so long that I instinctively run through this framework in my head as someone is explaining a potential deal to me. It's become a part of my wiring now, so I tend to do a SWOT analysis on every decision, whether it's business, personal, relational, or any other part of my life. What's cool about the SWOT method is that it isn't just a pro/con list about the issue at hand; rather, it focuses specifically on me in relation to the decision. What are *my* strengths? What are *my* weaknesses, opportunities, and threats? By personalizing the decision to the unique individual (or business), the SWOT method helps you put all your cards on the table.

As you work toward getting a clear picture of where you want to go and where you are right now, let's take a good look at each of these four areas.

What Are Your Strengths?

Everybody is good at something. Even the most self-doubting, nervous, quiet person has an abundance of strengths that can (and should) be used to make a difference in the world, both personally and professionally.

Depending on your personality style, this may be the most uncomfortable assignment I'll give you in this whole book, but here we go: I want you to take careful, thoughtful inventory of your strengths. All of them. And don't just think about them; write them down. This isn't an act of pride or bragging, so don't let any false humility get in your way. You aren't going to show this to anyone; this is just for you. Yes, it may be awkward for you, but you will never make much progress toward your goals—especially your finances—if you cannot take an honest evaluation of what you have to offer professionally, personally, relationally, financially, and in every other area.

Now, what does a strength look like? It's not that complicated. Are you reasonably good at your job? That's a strength. Do you have a good personality? That's a strength. Do you have friends? Do you have any money? Do people like you? Do you have people at home and at work who are invested in your success? Do you have an education? Are you skilled at what you do for a living? Are you skilled at what you do for fun? Do you have an idea that's unique? Do you have quality connections in your network? Are you good with computers? Do you have personal experience with the issue at hand? Do you have the desire to achieve? Are you willing to go the extra mile? Do you know where to look for answers and support? These are all strengths, and, believe it or not, not everybody has them in the same proportion—but everyone has strengths.

These things seem so basic, but it always amazes me how often people discount their strengths. They say things like, "I'm not good at anything" or, "I don't have anything going for me." If you allow yourself to believe that, you will lose the fight before you ever step into the ring. You're throwing in the towel. Sure, you may go through the motions, but you won't win. How could you? You're telling everyone right from the start that you have nothing to offer. If *you* don't believe in you, why should anyone else?

I knew a guy several years ago who had a serious self-esteem problem. He had dropped out of high school due to some family issues and started working with an older friend who had started a small plumbing company. I met him a few years later. By then, this guy was really down on himself. He was in his early twenties and had a bleak outlook on his life. He regretted dropping out of school and felt like he'd never make anything of himself without a college degree, which, at that point, seemed impossible. One day he told me, "I screwed my life up big-time, man. I can't do anything right."

Funny thing is, he was fixing a complex plumbing issue in my house at the time. I said, "What are you talking about? Look at what you're doing right now! I have no idea how any of this stuff works, but you're doing it better, faster, and cheaper than any other plumber in town could!"

"Great," he whined. "I guess I'll be unclogging drains for the rest of my life."

I yelled, "That sounds *awesome!* You could be the best plumber in the area. Do you have any idea how valuable your skills are to people?" Then it dawned on me: he really didn't. He had no idea how good he was or how important that skill and experience are to others. "Besides," I continued, "you've been shadowing your boss for years now. You don't just know how to do the plumbing; you know how to run a plumbing business. What if you started your own company? You could be the most sought-after plumber and plumbing company in the state!"

I saw the light flicker behind his eyes. He'd spent years kicking himself for everything he'd done wrong and had totally missed the fact that he had developed an incredibly valuable skill set, reputation, and network of people who would love to see him succeed. Once he identified these strengths, his whole demeanor changed. It was like looking at a different person.

I will say it again: you are *great* at something, and you have a *lot* going for you. Never doubt that. So when it comes to growing your financial pie, what are your strengths? What are you good at? Don't read any farther until you're able to answer that.

What Are Your Weaknesses?

Once you have identified your strengths, you need to switch gears and take a good look at your weaknesses. Again, this is not complicated. If a strength is something that's working *for* you, a weakness is anything that's working *against* you. Some people stink at managing or making money. Others have an irritating personality that gets in the way of personal connections. Some have social anxiety. Some have poor organizational, management, communication, or networking skills. Some talk too much. Some don't talk enough. Some are broke. Some don't have any quality networking connections. Some are bad with computers. Some are unskilled with accounting. Marketing scares some people. No matter how many strengths you have and how much you have going for you, you definitely have some weaknesses that you must identify and either improve or work around. If you don't, success will always feel ten times harder than it has to. Learning what you don't know or where you need help is the second step most people don't take; they want to enjoy their strengths and act like they don't have weaknesses.

As I've used the SWOT analysis on myself and others over the years, I've noticed an interesting connection between people's strengths and their weaknesses. Oftentimes, a weakness can be the flip side of the person's strength. We see this all the time: The executive who successfully leads a billion-dollar company but who can't lead his own family. The marriage counselor who's been divorced three times. The economics professor who's flat broke. The professional speaker who's great on stage but can't carry a five-minute conversation one-on-one. If you are having trouble identifying your weaknesses, just take a look at your list of strengths and ask yourself, *How might this strength be working against me? Is being good in this area blinding me to a weakness in another area?* Chances are, this will reveal a few weaknesses you might not have considered. For example, many people who are good at making money have no idea how to hang on to it, and the cash leaves as fast as it comes.

I've heard many speakers and authors suggest you ask the people who are closest to you to help identify your weaknesses. You can try that, but I've found loved ones are more likely to lie to you or excuse your shortcomings because they also know and admire your strengths. Besides, they probably love you and would rather lie than hurt your feelings. If you really want to get an outside opinion, you might try a radical approach and ask your enemies or competition what *they* think your weaknesses are. These people may *love* the invitation to tell you what they think of you! This doesn't have to be torture though. In fact, our enemies can be tremendous sources of insight and opportunity.

Just a few weeks ago, I got a call out of the blue from a guy I've done business with several times before. This is *not* a friend. The truth is, he doesn't like me, and I don't like him. We've tried, but we simply do not get along. He was calling because he wanted to bring me into a deal he was working on. That may sound odd to you. Why would a guy who doesn't particularly like me bring me a good business opportunity? It was because he *knew* me—my strengths and my weaknesses. He had identified a weakness of his own, and he knew I had strengths that compensated for his weaknesses. It wasn't even difficult for him to make the call. He knew we'd have a better chance of getting the deal done *together* than he would have had without me. We're in the final stages of that deal right now, and we'll both make millions off it. But we still don't enjoy spending time with each other.

We are certainly civil, but we won't crave more time with each other after our business dealings are complete.

This demonstrates another major point about our weaknesses that I'll come back to a few times throughout this book: a weakness isn't a roadblock; it's simply a diversion. It doesn't stop me in my tracks; it simply means I need to find a different route. When you identify your weaknesses and know what to watch out for, you can prepare yourself for the obstacles that stand between you and your goal. That gives you the chance to either

1. Figure out a creative way through (or around) the problem.
2. Partner with someone else whose strengths make up for your weaknesses.

No one is good at everything, so the best teams are made up of people whose strengths compensate for others' weaknesses. These can be some of the best partnerships you'll ever have in your personal and professional life, and it's possible only when you take the time to identify the good, the bad, and the ugly about yourself. You should really make an effort to appreciate the differences because—as much as they can be helpful—they are also a potential source of friction.

Before I move on, I want to correct a common misconception about our weaknesses. It is incredibly easy to put 10 percent of our focus on our strengths and the other 90 percent on correcting or strengthening a weakness. This is something we learn as little kids. If your child handed you a report card with five As and one D, what would your reaction be? If you're like most parents, you'd gloss over the As and put all your attention on the D. "What happened? Were you not paying attention? Do you need a tutor? Can you do extra credit? Can you retake the class? Were you just lazy?" If one of my boys randomly flunked a class, I know those are the thoughts that would go through my head.

When we identify a weakness, our instinct is often to put more time and effort into overcoming that shortcoming. But let's be real: you will never turn a weakness into a strength. Yes, you can get a little better at something. You can make marginal improvements. But it will never become a strength and will likely never be something you enjoy. So why waste so much blood, sweat, and tears trying to bring your competency level up from *completely* horrible to *mostly* horrible? You'll get exponentially more bang for your buck if you pour all that effort and intentionality into making your strengths *even stronger*. These are the things you're naturally gifted at and likely enjoy doing. You can't help but grow in your strengths as you spend time developing them. As for your weaknesses, that's the value in partnering with others to create a cohesive, well-rounded team that can overcome any obstacle and achieve any victory.

What Are Your Opportunities?

Money is always looking for opportunity. In fact, I'll be so bold as to say that the easiest resource in the world to get your hands on is money. If you've traditionally struggled to make money or raise capital for your projects, you may think I'm blowing smoke right now, but I'm dead serious. Whenever I make that statement to a class of finance students, every hand in the room goes up, either with a question or an objection. I can tell right then and there which students will be successful. It's the ones with a question. When you accept the notion that money is an easily accessible resource, you'll start "finding" money everywhere. When you see it as a scarcity, you'll always be blind to it. But that's not money's fault. It isn't society's fault or culture's fault. And you can't blame it on sexism, racism, or any of the other "isms" people talk about so often. Remember when I said earlier that "it's your fault"? Well, this is a prime example. If you can't put your hands on some money, it's because you're approaching finances with a scarcity mindset—and that will always blind you to the resources that are all around you.

Money is active. It flows from one thing to another. That's why they call it *cash flow*. Financial author and radio host Dave Ramsey likes to say, "Money flows *from* those who can't manage it *to* those who can." I like that concept because it shows that money—and money's availability—isn't the problem. The problem is the hands that money is in.

Imagine money as a tool. Like any tool, it can't do anything on its own; it requires competent hands to wield it. In my experience, competent people *already* have ideas that need funding, so when money flows to that person, he can put it right to work. Most people get this backward and think money itself is the opportunity. No! Instead, money has a way of finding people who are ready to put it to work. For example, I heard the other day that the United States is looking to sell ten thousand diesel buses that are no longer being used. Immediately, I went to work coming up with a plan to buy them, put them on a freighter, and sell them in China, where they are in high demand. I didn't start with the money; I started with the opportunity. If the opportunity is good and I've planned it well, I know I can find the money.

I said earlier that there's an estimated $5 trillion just sitting in money market accounts in the United States today. As far as I'm concerned, that money represents $5 trillion in unfunded opportunities. Money doesn't want to sit on a shelf; it wants to be used! All it's waiting for is a person with an idea, a plan, some passion, and a compelling argument. If someone with all of that but no money came to me, I could solve the money problem for them in a heartbeat—and create more money for myself in the process. So why are people "hiding" their money from people like me who have more opportunities than we know what to do with? Fear. People waste opportunity because they're afraid of loss. They'd rather choose a "safe" 1 percent return with a bank than taking more risk on an opportunity that could bring them 12 percent or more. Even Jesus argued against this mindset!

In the parable of the talents, Jesus tells the story of a rich man who left town for a while and gave a pile of money to three of his servants to manage in his absence. He gave different sums to each according to how well the servants managed money. He gave one guy five bags of gold, which the servant invested and doubled. He gave another servant two bags of gold, which he also invested and doubled. And he gave the third servant one bag of gold. This servant was terrified of risk. He was afraid his boss would punish him if he lost the money, so he dug a hole and buried it. When the boss came back, he was furious that this servant was too scared to even put it in the bank to earn a little interest. In the end, the rich man took the bag of gold back from the scared servant and gave it to the one who now had ten bags. In today's terms, we could say he emptied this guy's savings account and gave all the money to the guy who invested in growth stocks or businesses!

Jesus ends the story by telling the crowd that whoever has a lot will be given more and whoever has a little will probably lose what little they have. Some people despise that lesson. They use it to fuel the idea that the rich get richer while the poor get poorer, and they moan about "equity" and how "unfair" the system is. But I don't think Jesus is making a statement about the system; I think he's talking about the natural flow of money. People who aren't scared to jump on opportunities—even though there's risk—will naturally have more money than those who are. No risk, no reward. It's just the way it is. You can try to change that through taxation and government policies aimed at "leveling the playing field" or making the wealthy "pay their fair share," but you cannot legislate opportunity. If the government waved a magic wand tomorrow and completely evened out every American's bank balance so everyone had the same amount of money, things wouldn't stay even for long. Almost immediately, you'd see the people who were rich before building wealth again, and you'd see the people who were broke before starting to lose what the government gave them. Why? Because it's not about the money. It's about the ability to see and seize opportunity, and that's a life skill that will never be equally distributed across all people.

Now, you may be asking, *How does all this help me see the opportunities in front of me today?* Easy: this gives you permission to totally forget about money for now. People let money—or the lack of money—blind them to the opportunities all around them. When you take off those blinders, though, you can see opportunity everywhere. Not long ago, for example, I was sitting in a deck chair by the pool at a resort in the Bahamas. It was one year into COVID-19, and the hotel was still short-staffed and operating at limited capacity. You know what I was thinking while sitting out by the pool in paradise? *I bet I could get a good deal on this place if I tried to buy it right now.* I wasn't thinking about where I'd get the money; I was thinking about the opportunity literally right in front of my face. I was at a beautiful resort that had been losing money due to the pandemic for over a year. It was an unprecedented opportunity to buy up some pristine resort locations. I knew the people would be back before long. As far as I was concerned, this resort was on sale! Whether or not I end up buying it, the point is that I could see the opportunity. If it's a good idea, the money will be there. And if I can't put the funds together this time, that's okay too. I have plenty of ideas and an eye for opportunity. No need to cry when one doesn't work out.

I want to be as clear as possible here because there is so much confusion around this issue: money is *not* an opportunity. Money is a resource; it *funds* opportunities. Very few people want money for the sake of having money. Rather, they want the things that money can pay for—things like nice stuff, building a business, hiring a new employee, exciting experiences, and a secure retirement. And just because I've made it clear that money is freely available if you know where and how to look for it, that doesn't mean you can simply sit back and wait for it to flow your way. It doesn't work like that. You still have to pound the pavement, make connections, build a network, and do the work of finding where that money is hiding. Build the idea and the vison first, and then look for the money, people, and resources later. Ideas attract money, and money is on the hunt. As I've said before, the harder I work, the luckier I get! I'll talk more about how and where to find money later in the book.

What Are Your Threats?

Last, we come to identifying your threats. The title of this book, *Who's Eating Your Pie?*, makes an assumption: someone is trying to take your money and/or your time. It's an absolute certainty. If that weren't true, I would have called the book *Is Someone Eating Your Pie?* It isn't a happy thought, but the fact remains that you will always be defending your money from people, systems, and organizations who are trying to take it. I don't want to make you completely paranoid—but I do want to make you a *little* paranoid. If you can't see the threats to your success, you'll never be able to defend yourself.

Who are your threats when it comes to defending your pie? There are the obvious dangers, of course, such as taxes, unwise spending, overpaying for purchases, and credit card interest rates. But there are many more you probably have never considered. We tend to stop at surface-level thinking when we're naming our threats, but I want to challenge you to dig deeper. When you do, you'll unearth many more threats than you ever imagined.

For example, I recently talked to a man who owns a chain of gas stations. When I was a kid, a gas station was *just* a gas station. There was a line of pumps with a tiny, usually run-down shack of a building sitting next to them. The only reason a customer would ever go inside was to either pay or use the bathroom. Even then, the bathrooms were usually located outside the main building, so you had to get the key from the attendant, walk around to the back of the building, and find an often-neglected and dirty restroom. Nowadays, things are much different. Gas stations are basically little grocery stores with custom coffee bars, hot food, and large (indoor) restrooms. The gas tanks often seem like an afterthought, as most of the owner's profit comes from what's sold *inside* the building rather than out at the pumps.

I asked this guy about his business and who his biggest threats were. He stroked his chin and said, "My threats? Well, that would be anyone who sells gas. Anyone who sells hot food. Anyone who has a car wash. Anyone who has a bathroom. Anyone who sells snacks and soft drinks. Donut shops. Fast-food restaurants. Drug stores. Grocery stores. Walmart. Souvenir shops. Banks [because of what he makes on the ATM]. Liquor stores. I guess pretty much every other business anywhere near me is a threat. I cut into all of those businesses in one way or another, so I guess *everyone* is a threat to me."

He made such a great point that I started teaching this perspective whenever I guest lecture in college classes. I tell the students, "Imagine you're a business called You Company. Everyone who's not you is a potential threat to You Company—even your employees." When you run a business, even if you have great relationships with your employees, you still have to defend yourself against them in some way. You'll always be doing this little dance where they're trying to get the most money possible for the least amount of work. You, of course, want to give them the least money possible for the greatest amount of work. It's not that either of you want to harm the other party; it's just that you're each defending your money from the other.

With this in mind, I challenge you to take some time to write down anyone and anything that is a threat to your success. Who and what is trying to eat your pie? Your limiting thoughts? Your spending? Your coworkers? Your competitors? Your employees? Your taxes? Your relationships? Lack of planning? If anyone or anything is wasting your income or time, write it down. And remember, this is a list of *threats*, not *enemies*. I'm not suggesting there's any malice or ill will involved. The goal here isn't to cut these people and organizations out of your life; rather, the only goal is to recognize all the different ways others affect your financial success. In some ways, I look to give others more money each year, once I have aligned their interest with mine or my companies' objectives and established a reward system that shares additional financial gain earned solely by the employees' efforts. I want the employees who really help us to earn more money working for me than anywhere else. It's amazing how much of a difference aligning interests makes in business dealings. They will work smarter and watch expenses more closely if they share in the savings or the additional profits. Make everyone feel like an owner. Even though they are not actual owners of the business, they can own their job.

PLOTTING YOUR COURSE

We started this chapter with two critical questions:

1. Where do you want to end up?
2. Where are you right now?

The first question comes down to your goals, something we'll discuss in more detail throughout this book. The second question requires an intentional, critical self-evaluation to identify where you are, how you're doing, what you're working with, and what you're working against. When you know those things—your strengths, weaknesses, opportunities, and threats—you can see your current position on the GPS. Only then can you plot a course to your destination.

SECTION 2

PLANNING
FINANCIAL
SUCCESS

CHAPTER 5

What's Stopping You?

*I*n the previous chapter, we looked at identifying where you want to go. With that target in mind, let me now ask you, what's stopping you from getting there?

We've already seen how guilt or a depressed self-image can get in our way and prevent us from even identifying where we are and where we want to go, but there are three other big, emotional blockers that stop us in our tracks. You can picture these things as three grim reapers standing ready to strike down your dreams and crush you if left unchecked. Even worse, if you allow these destructive thoughts to run rampant through your life, they'll wipe out any sense of joy or satisfaction from *every* part of your life—not just your money. Your success in all areas depends on your ability to face down these devilish blockers once and for all. So, let's do it.

BLOCKER #1: FEAR

Nothing has stolen more joy, rotted more relationships, killed more careers, or prevented more wealth building than fear. Nothing. Fear is Public Enemy #1 when it comes to achieving your goals and getting where you want to go.

We are afraid of everything—afraid of failure, regret, shame, self-loathing, disappointment, jealousy, resentment, and even afraid of our own success. Yes, you heard me correctly: many people are afraid of success. Somehow people are almost more comfortable with the subtle comfort of low expectations than the high bar of success. Then we allow that false comfort to cover up the high price we pay for failure. Failure becomes a blanket we hide under, like a child in bed hiding from the monster in the closet. We often let that "comfortable" fear stop us from doing what we need to do to advance our goals. We shrug our shoulders, say something like, "Why bother?," and then plop down in front of the TV to mindlessly zone out for three hours before bed. Three hours that could have been spent planning, dreaming, and building. Three hours that could have taken you ten steps closer to your goal. Three hours that you could have either used or wasted, and you chose to waste them. Now is the time to make different choices and begin choosing to be productive and careful with your time.

How often do we excuse the time-wasting activities in our lives by convincing ourselves we *need* or *deserve* a break? Sure, that's true sometimes—but not nearly as often as we tell ourselves. Most of those times, we aren't relaxing; we're just hiding.

We are afraid of looking stupid, so we hold back. We don't speak up. We don't take the big risk. We'd rather stay where we are than take a leap that could either take us to the next level or drop us flat on our faces. We get so caught up in appearances, trying to show everyone how calm, cool, and collected we are, when the truth is nobody is looking at us anyway. I've said it before and I'll say it again: *no one cares!* Everyone's got their hands full with their own lives; they aren't wasting their time thinking about you. Most of the people you know have no idea how well or how poorly you're doing. And if you struck gold or went broke tomorrow, it would barely be a blip on their radar. In fact, over time it might not even be a blip on yours. Most of the time, the failure we try so hard to avoid wouldn't amount to a stumble in the scope of our whole life. In fact, most of the risk you will ever take is *perceived* risk, not *genuine* risk. That is, the risk is mainly in your mind rather than in your circumstances.

Afraid to Dream

People are afraid to dream because they're afraid to fail. They're told by a parent that they "can't do it" or that they'll "never amount to anything." They're convinced that they don't have the education, intelligence, courage, or personality to bring their dreams to life. It would have been so easy for my parents to fall into this trap with me when I started stuttering. Once it became clear that my stutter was a part of my life for the long haul, Mom and Dad could have coddled me, speaking fear and failure into my life under the guise of kindness. They could have said, "Erik, your stutter is going to keep you from doing some things. You should probably set your sights a little lower, son. It's OK. It's not your fault." Even typing that freaks me out!

In an attempt to minimize my discomfort, they could have guided me to being a recluse who did not verbally engage with people often. It was awful to stutter every single time I met someone and watch them become uncomfortable for me as I struggled to spit out words. I thank God my parents did just the opposite. They didn't let me hide from the world; instead, they set me up with a lemonade stand where I was *forced* to talk to people. But they also made sure I had a reward for my hard work; every time someone bought a cup of lemonade, I got paid. At the end of the day, I was more excited about my eighty dollars than I was frustrated about my stutter. From age five, I associated reward with effort. Even today, when I make much more than eighty dollars per day, I still look for those tangible and intangible rewards for my effort—and I look for ways to reward others for theirs.

But how many parents send these kinds of high-fear, low-expectation messages to their children? Out of a sense of practicality, parents say things like "Be realistic" or, "Get your head out of the clouds" when their rambunctious little kids start spouting off all the great, big, huge, wonderful things they're going to do in life. And, with every "helpful" bit of real-world, practical advice, the parent blurs their children's ability to see their full potential and cripples them with fear. Alternatively, telling someone they are great at something when they are not is also discouraging in the long run. We live in a globalized society. Just because you are the best basketball player on your street doesn't mean you're ready to suit up for the NBA. Encouraging and helpful feedback is the balance to seek when giving feedback. For example, if your child is a runner, you might say, "Son, you are doing well, and I am proud of you no matter what you choose to do. However, if you want to make the Olympics, you need to drop six seconds off of your time. Let's explore ways to make that happen."

A sense of adventure is lost on today's society. Young adults are trapped inside of these little plastic, protective bubbles their parents stuck them in at a young age. They've been protected from failure for so long that they have no idea how to take a hit. But we *need* to know how to fail. We need to know that a fall may hurt, but it usually won't kill us. We need to know what it feels like to fall short of a goal. We need to learn that broken bones, broken hearts, and broken spirits can and will heal over time. If we never experience pain, we never get to understand how powerful a motivator pain can be. Pain is an excellent motivator in life; fear is not.

Afraid in the Face of Opportunity

The times in my life when I've been most afraid of something are the times when I've been right at the edge of my biggest, boldest opportunities. As the stakes increase, so does the fear. It's a natural response. But it doesn't have to control us. In fact, we can learn to control *it*. Babe Ruth stepped up to the plate and pointed his bat where he was going to hit the ball. Muhammad Ali spent weeks before a boxing match talking trash about his opponent and even predicted the round when he'd knock the guy out. These legends knew how to leverage other's fear for their own gain. When anyone else would be terrified, these guys projected absolute confidence. That confidence—the apparent absence of fear—messes with people. Ali's predictions would get in his opponents' heads. They'd hear him say, "Going down in round 3" over and over until they fixated on round 3. How do you think they felt when the bell dinged to mark the start of the third round during the actual fight? He used their fear against them, and he won. Power over fear gives you power over people and circumstances. You can create a new reality by pushing back on fear and using it to your advantage.

I'm speaking from experience here. I know exactly what it's like to let fear get in my way. In 2005, I was thirty-eight years old and living in California. I'd been making about $1 million a year for the past decade, and I wanted to spread my wings a bit and try something new. Some real estate investor buddies and I stumbled upon a trailer park that was for sale. I dug into the details and saw some serious profit potential in redeveloping the land for an attached housing development. After a ton of research and due diligence, I excitedly jumped into the deal with my friends, we each put up some money and guaranteed a huge loan, and we got to work. After all, it was California housing. What could go wrong?!

It took a few years to complete, which took us into 2008. You may remember that 2008 was *not* a good year for real estate. Our development was wrapping up just as "The Great Recession" was ramping up. Our property had lost around 40 percent of its value before we even had the first unit ready for sale. Even worse, banks had stopped lending on attached housing, so there was practically no chance of selling any of our units for a long time. When we started the project, we estimated a profit approaching $10 million to split between us. But by the time we finished, we had lost everything we put into the deal *plus* we were millions short on repaying the bank loans. It's difficult to describe the sinking feeling of watching your project fall in value over 40 percent in less than a year. Every night I'd lie in bed and think of alternatives. Could we make them apartments and rent them out until the market stabilized?

That strategy would have worked, but the bank said, "We are not partners. We are lenders, and we want to be paid back on time." The bank was in the driver's seat, and as I sit here some decade or so later, I realize the apartment conversion would have not only saved us millions, it would have made us over $20 million by now. But instead, we learned the borrower is not in control and that timing is everything.

We eventually unloaded the whole development through an auction process by selling our units to over thirty individual cash buyers. One of my partners declared bankruptcy. Another cut his losses and exited after paying $250,000 toward the total loss out of a home equity loan. And the remaining almost $5 million was split between me and another guarantor. I learned what "jointly and severally liable" means, and that the word *guarantee* is one of the most expensive words in the English language.

A couple of years earlier I had been excited about enjoying all the upside in exchange for "only" guaranteeing the loan. I remember thinking, *You mean all I have to do for my ownership percentage is put in a little cash and guarantee a loan? No problem!* After all, the building partner had done this for over twenty years and had *never* had a deal fall apart. I felt this opportunity was almost too good to be true. Flash forward a few years, and I was personally stuck holding millions in losses. Oh, and did I mention this was the first big deal I ever personally guaranteed? What a mess.

Coming through that ordeal, I had many people who started speaking fear into my life under the guise of helpful, practical advice. "This should be a lesson to you," they said. "This is what happens when you step outside of your day-to-day expertise." Were they right? Yes and no. Yes, this *is* what can happen to you when you take big swings. You can miss. You can fall and fail. You can end up broke. But is this what *always* happens? Are those failures always fatal? Absolutely not.

Failure is fatal only if you quit—and I'm not a quitter. If you're still reading, you're not either!

I recovered for five years as I paid back everything I owed from that disaster. Then I was ready to try again. I learned to begin with the end in sight and to go into deals only if I had a clear exit, sort of like not going into a tunnel unless you see daylight out the other side. I played future deals a bit more cautiously, and we had great success. I had a big win, then another, and then another. My confidence grew each time I faced the fear, even the times when the deal didn't work out. Now, looking back on twenty years of those types of big-swing deals, I can see some losses, but there have been many more winners. I'm living a life I never imagined these days, and it's all because I didn't let fear blind me to my own potential. Dare to dream, then put legs under your dreams.

Remember, fear wants to steal your opportunities. If you take a big swing, sure, you may miss. That's a risk. But at least you'll come away from the ordeal with some experience and knowledge you can use to do better the next time. That's why I call these things *setbacks* instead of *failures*. A setback is only temporary. It's a painful lesson but one I can leverage for bigger, better deals moving forward. But what does set us up for total failure? Not taking a swing at all. You will absolutely miss the ball every time you don't swing the bat. In other words, there's a 100 percent chance of failure every time you back away from an opportunity. When we allow fear to steal our opportunities, we are surrendering our chance for a better, bigger, bolder, more impactful life. We become so scared of a setback that we accept failure. In doing so, we allow fear to steal the *whole* pie.

Fear and Action

If you ever hope to see yourself clearly and, just as importantly, see the incredible opportunities ahead of you, you've got to wipe the fear from your eyes. I'm not suggesting you ignore it completely; I think fear can be wonderfully instructive at times. Instead, I suggest taking on a healthy view of fear. Recognize it. Learn from it. Tip your hat to it. Thank it for what it's trying to show you. Then find a workaround to solve the problem. Deals are like life: they're all full of knowns and unknowns. Figure out a way to solve the known problems and leave margin for the unknown issues that will certainly arise. And don't assume the unknowns are all negative! Sometimes the unknown can be a major blessing, like Amazon moving their headquarters to an area where you already own some real estate. So do the hard work in advance, buckle up, and become a problem-solver as you move along through life.

You want to know what the difference is between a successful person's and an unsuccessful person's view of fear? Unsuccessful people view fear as a great, big chance for a loss and therefore never take action; in contrast, successful people view fear as an opportunity to solve a problem and are afraid *not* to take action once they have found a solution. Men and women who change the world have learned how to conquer their fears, and that doesn't mean learning to be fearless; it just means learning how to take action despite the fear and finding ways to solve problems. When fear is trying to keep you from doing something, sometimes the best you can do is to do it scared—once you have spent the time solving the major issues.

BLOCKER #2: BAD EXPECTATIONS

The second big blocker that often prevents us from getting where we want to go—or steals our joy once we get there—is bad expectations.

I've been blessed to get to know dozens of Navy SEALs over the years. These are hands-down the toughest, bravest guys I've ever met. In the military, these are the best of the best, the elite warriors who get the job done no matter what that job entails. The first SEAL I ever met shared all sorts of harrowing stories about his life on the battle-field. Some of what he told me sounded like it came straight out of a movie. I couldn't believe what I was hearing! When he noticed the disbelief on my face, he smirked and said, "Erik, Navy SEALs are the best in the world. We can do anything—as long as you tell us up front what to expect."

He explained that the only times things ever went sideways for him were the rare times when his intel was incorrect or incomplete. For example, his mission brief may say something like, "We're dropping a team of five SEALs in *this* location. You'll free one hostage, who is being held *here*. There are three hostiles in the building who are posted *here*, *here*, and *here*." That may sound like an easy mission if you were playing *Call of Duty* on PlayStation, but, of course, it's much more hazardous in real life. These guys drop into hot spots like this all the time, armed with not only their training and weapons but also their expectations of how the mission will go. If the expectations are way off—say there are ten hostiles instead of three—then the whole plan goes out the window. That's when they have to start improvising, and that's where things can go very wrong very quickly.

That's how it is in our lives too. The stakes may not be life or death, but the principle is similar. We can generally handle whatever life throws at us as long as we see it coming; the surprise hits, however, can take us out hard and fast. In life, business, relationships, and money, expectations are everything. We plan for the future based on what we know today. When our vision is blurred due to negative self-talk, guilt, fear, or any of the other things we've discussed, we are basically making plans based on bad intel. They may look good on paper, but they'll fall apart in real life.

Expectations for a "Type" of Life

Sometimes, though, we can do everything right and still get caught off guard by the outcomes we get. I believe the reason most people aren't happy is because their expectations and their reality are so far apart. They spend so much time thinking about what they think their life will look like that they have a hard time accepting a different outcome—even if that outcome is better than they ever dreamed.

Expectations for Recognition

Our expectations also get in our way when we're looking for recognition and appreciation that just isn't coming. We work to please other people, but it's never enough. We try to get someone's attention, but it never comes. Parents keep waiting for their kids to wake up and realize how much Mom and Dad have done for them, but they rarely do. We pin all our happiness on what someone else might say to us or do for us later, but we just keep waiting. And waiting. And waiting. The hard truth is that most people aren't interested in what you're doing unless it benefits them directly. And even then, they're more interested in what they're *getting* than what you're *giving*.

A friend of mine who owns a highly successful company gave out bonuses one year that in most cases were greater than each employee's entire annual salary. He said of the 120 people to whom he handed millions of dollars, only two people came back and thanked him a second time when they opened the envelope and saw how much he had given them. That means 118 people most certainly *liked* the bonus, but they also probably *expected* it. They thought they deserved it.

The business took a downturn the very next year, and the new bonuses were considerably smaller. What do you think happened among the employees? After everyone had opened their envelopes, the same two people showed immense gratitude, and the other one hundred and eighteen whined about how small their bonuses were that year. They were expecting greater recognition, even though they knew their efforts hadn't been as productive that year. When their boss failed to deliver the recognition they thought they were entitled to, they grumbled about the size of the check he'd just given them. They were disappointed by the amount. He was disappointed in their reactions. Even though everyone walked away with a nice bonus, everyone—including my friend—felt as though they somehow lost.

I've got some bad news: you cannot expect another person to give you a sense of success, purpose, satisfaction, and accomplishment. Everyone else is too focused on their own lives to notice yours.

You may expect them to shower you with praise all day long, but the reality is . . . they won't.

BLOCKER #3: COMPARISON LIVING

If you're under age thirty, there's a good chance you've lived your entire life online, probably enhanced by studio-quality photo filters. As such, in today's social media–driven world, it is almost impossible not to be distracted—if not outright dominated—by what your so-called friends and followers have. People just *love* to show off online, from new homes to cars, from vacations to sweet sixteen blowouts, from beach photos to pouty-lipped "candid" selfies. Keeping up with the Joneses has never been more prevalent—and impossible.

The problem is, comparing your life to someone else's is one of the most demotivating, success-blocking things you can do. We scroll through our social feeds and think, *I wish I had her life*. But her "perfect" life is probably anything but perfect. It's not real. We aren't chasing what someone else has; we're chasing the lie someone else is telling. Worse, if *everyone* does this, no one is pursuing their own dreams. I chase what you have. You chase what he has. He chases what she has. It's a vicious cycle going nowhere. As Theodore Roosevelt said, "Comparison is the thief of joy." And that was *before* the age of Instagram and Twitter. My Aunt Ruby put it another way, "Honey, if you knew their problems, you would keep your own."

Celebrate Other's Success

So, how does comparison living block our personal success? For one, I think we have lost the ability to celebrate others' success. The more we see inside someone else's life, the more we want what they have. Call it jealousy, envy, discontentment, or plain old greed, but something in us turns our noses up when we see someone else winning—especially if we don't think they deserve it.

This self-serving attitude was (literally) kicked out of me at a young age. I was fortunate to attend one of Chuck Norris's karate studios. Yes, *that* Chuck Norris. This is a man who deserves the huge following and fan base he's built over the decades—not because of his martial artistry, action movies, or success on TV, but because of his heart. Everyone associated with Chuck Norris's karate method knows his twelve-point Code of Conduct by heart. It was posted on the walls of his studios, and every student had to memorize it. Four points that always stood out to me were:

- I will look for the good in all people and make them feel worthwhile.
- If I have nothing good to say about a person, I will say nothing.
- I will give so much time to the improvement of myself that I will have no time to criticize others.
- I will be as enthusiastic about the success of others as I am about my own success.

I learned these lessons in the early 1980s, but how much more important are they today?

The phones in our pockets broadcast the most intimate details of our friends' lives, things my parents couldn't imagine sharing for themselves or seeing from others. Sometimes it can feel like we've got a front-row seat to a parade someone else is leading for themselves. I understand the gut reaction to either look away, turn your nose up, or question whether that person deserves it. But I want to suggest an alternative reaction: join the parade. Celebrate your friend's success. As Chuck Norris would say, be as enthusiastic about their success as you are about your own. Their success shouldn't threaten you. You should be focused on the size of your own pie. You simply can't grow your pie if you spend all your time worried about someone else's.

Be the Best You, Not a Second-Rate Someone Else

I would love my five sons to follow me into the business I've built, making it a true family enterprise. But if that's not what they want to do, it would likely wreck not only the business but, potentially our relationships. I tell my boys all the time, "Live, love, laugh, forgive, and follow *your* dreams." I have also told them on occasion, "You can be either an excellent *you* or a horrible *me*." That is, we can only be ourselves and be our very best when we are living out our own passions in our own ways. It would be ridiculous for me to force them to come into the business and do things "my way or the highway." My way is just that: it's *my way*. It's not theirs. If they spend their lives trying to become me, they'll fail—both at being me and at being themselves. It's a lose-lose scenario, and it's one that can crush their spirits and leave them in a life they don't even like, let alone love.

I have strengths my sons don't have. They have strengths I don't have. There are areas I'm weak in where they excel and vice versa. It's foolish for them to try to squash their unique talents, giftedness, and perspective in order to become poor clones of me. The world already has me; what it needs now is five other Weir men who are each wonderfully unique and equipped to make their own impact on the world.

The same is true when we see someone else's success and attempt to get what they have by doing what they've done. What works for one person may not work for another. In fact, it probably won't. Truly successful people don't follow someone else's road map to the letter. Instead, they learn the overarching lessons and apply them in their own unique way. Think mentorship, not duplication. Otherwise, we lose sight not only of where we're going but of who we are.

When I'm out with friends, for example, I sometimes hear an amateur performer sing karaoke. The person behind the microphone may do their best to sound like Chris Stapleton, but it usually isn't even close. Even if someone nails the notes, the performance overall feels . . . empty. Why? Because I've seen Chris Stapleton perform; the karaoke version is just a poor imitation at best. But when someone like Stapleton covers another artist's song, he doesn't try to imitate the other singer. Instead, he makes the song *his own*. He reinvents it by putting his own unique stamp on it. That's the difference between art and imitation. Artists use their unique giftedness to create something new; imitators hide their true selves and act like clones of someone else. And of all the multimillionaires and billionaires I know, I've never met one who's content to simply copy what everyone else is doing.

HOW TO PUSH PAST THE OBSTACLES

Now that we've called out fear, bad expectations, and comparing ourselves to other people as three huge success blockers, how do we deal with them? I've got three suggestions.

Step 1: Own Everything

The first step to pushing past the obstacles that stand between you and success is to open your eyes, take a really good look at who you are, what you're doing, and what you want, and then own it. Own your mistakes, success, ambition, and failures. This is *your* life, and these are *your* circumstances. Own everything about it. Even if someone else is responsible for the mess, you still have to own it as part of your life. In other words, you have to play the hand you were dealt; you can't just throw your cards on the table and quit the game.

People get into trouble when they don't own their lives. If there is something in your life you'd like to change, then change it. If there's something in your life that other people say you should change but you don't want to, then just say no. Don't agree with them and then continually whine about what you *should* do if you don't really want to do it. Say you're a bartender at the local pub. Your friends—bankers, real estate agents, doctors, lawyers, and so on—are constantly encouraging you to get a "better" job. However, you really like where you work. You enjoy the steady stream of customers to talk to, you like working nights, you like being an active part of your community, your income supports a lifestyle you enjoy, and you love being able to clock out and leave your work behind at the end of the night. You know what that sounds like to me? It sounds like a happy person.

If you were in that position, why would you think you need to make a change? Because your friends say you should? Forget that.

You've got to live your own life, and that means you get to choose your own level of aspiration and success. It may sound trite in a book about taking risk and financial success, but success comes in all forms and all sizes. You came into this world holding nothing, and you will exit the same way. So enjoy the ride. The joy is the process, not the destination.

Of course, I'm not saying you shouldn't have higher aspirations and goals. I'm just saying that you shouldn't stress yourself out and potentially ruin your life reaching for something you don't really want or need. If you want something more, then set some goals and get to work. If you are happy where you are, then give yourself permission to enjoy it without beating yourself up over needing to change. If you have completely wrecked your life with bad decisions and toxic relationships, own those things and make a plan for getting out of the hole you've put yourself in. The beautiful thing about life is that we get to choose who and what we want to be. Recognizing that fact—and owning it—enables you to see yourself more clearly than ever before.

Step 2: Look for Opportunities Where Others See Limits

We've already seen how some people see opportunities where other people see limitations. I'd like to add one more thought to that concept: you get to choose which kind of person you want to be. People who look for opportunities aren't necessarily born that way; it's a decision they've made along their journey. You can make that same decision. It may not feel natural, and you'll most certainly be uncomfortable as you practice this new skill, but you can master it just as well as anyone else.

There will always be people who refuse to look for opportunity in difficult circumstances. These are the people who pulled all their money out of the stock market during the recession, which then kept them from riding the recovery wave to even greater heights afterward. They could see only the limitation—the recession—and couldn't wrap their heads around the possibility that things would improve. Some people just feel smarter when they point out all the potential risks and things that can go wrong. It's like they make their living pointing out potential problems. That is a perfect example of limitation-based thinking, and that is the kind of thinking that will derail any financial plans you ever make. If you make your plans without addressing your limitations, your level of success will always be limited. But if you choose to look for opportunities even in a crisis, you'll set yourself up to win big-time, even when everyone around you is losing.

For example, I have a friend we'll call Bill who built a business around DNA forensic testing. He's not a scientist; he's an entrepreneur. He didn't care a thing in the world about DNA testing until a friend of his, who is a police officer, mentioned the big backlog of DNA evidence they had due to the high price of forensic testing. Bill saw an opportunity in the limitation. He bought a testing machine and sold his services at a steep discount, first to individual police districts and district attorney offices, then to entire municipalities across a dozen states. By 2019, he owned several testing machines and had built an eight-figure business dipping his toes into an area that everyone else saw as a problem.

Then COVID-19 happened. Again, where most of the world saw a huge limitation, Bill saw opportunity. He had a hunch he could spin up a new business in the face of the pandemic, and he was right. After some experimentation and tweaking, he discovered his DNA testing machines could be modified into COVID-19 testing machines. He started making deals with many of the states he'd built a relationship with and became their exclusive provider of COVID testing. Then, as professional sports leagues were trying to figure out how to reopen, Bill made deals with the NFL, MLB, and NBA. In a year when the whole world basically shut down, Bill grew his business from $2 million a month to $200 million a month, creating thousands of jobs in the process. Bill also knows this is a blip on the radar, because COVID-19 won't be this big a problem forever. To keep all those thousands of people employed, he'll need a new idea. And I have no doubt he'll have one.

Bill is a perfect example of someone who looks for opportunity where others see limits. He didn't have to be a scientist or doctor to make this happen either. All it took was an idea—and a willingness to *power through* to the opportunity when everyone else was *pulling back* from the limitation.

Step 3: Apply the Laws of Focus and Attraction

Have you ever bought a new car and then immediately started seeing the same car everywhere you go? You'd swear you never noticed that model very often—until you bought one. Then, once you had a vested interest and started focusing on that kind of car, your eyes were opened, and you started seeing them everywhere.

That's a loose example of the Law of Focus and the Law of Attraction working together. Simply put, the Law of Focus says we begin moving toward whatever we focus on. That's why, when you were learning how to drive a car, you might have been warned that the car will naturally go wherever your eyes go. It's literally bound to your focus. Similarly, the Law of Attraction is a philosophy that says we tend to attract things into our lives based on our thoughts. If I'm focused on yellow cars, for example, I'll start seeing them wherever I go.

These "laws" may sound strange to you, but it's amazing how often I've seen them play out in my life. I may set my focus on a new construction project, for example. Then, out of nowhere, I start bumping into investors looking for a new venture, contractors looking for a new project, business owners looking for office space, bankers offering exceptional rates, and so on. Over the course of a few weeks, I could fill every role in my new project with people I meet "out of the blue."

Where do these people come from? Chances are, they're already all around you; you just don't see them yet because you haven't focused on your goal. Once you apply the power of focus, you'll see people crawling out of the woodwork to help you get there. This is why I've grown so comfortable jumping into big deals before having every single detail planned out. I know from experience that, once I start focusing on getting something done, I'll start tripping over the people and resources I need to make it happen. Focus is so important, in fact, that I'll spend a whole chapter later talking about how to focus your mind and daily routines around the key problems you need to solve.

A NEW WAY OF SEEING
THE WORLD (AND YOURSELF)

Over the past two chapters I've challenged you to identify where you are right now, where you want to go, what's stopping you from getting there, and how to push through those obstacles. This is how you achieve unusual success in this world, growing your financial pie while defending it from the people and systems that want to steal it. But achieving this level of success requires you to look at the world differently than most people—and differently than you've probably ever looked at it before. I worked with a guy several years ago who perfectly represents what can happen when you learn this skill.

I met Robert soon after he filed for bankruptcy. He was a real estate agent during the housing crash of 2007, and his business imploded. His sports car had been repossessed that very morning, and his washer and dryer had been hauled off the day before. He had his few remaining belongings crammed in his wife's car, and he was on his way to his in-laws' house, where he'd been forced to move with his wife and two small children after losing his home. Needless to say, Robert's life was a wreck.

I asked him if I could walk him through a little exercise. He agreed, so first I set the stage for him, trying to reframe his perception of where he was at that moment in his life. He was a successful residential real estate agent who sold tons of homes—until he didn't. His income had literally dropped to nothing due to the recession, and he was starting at ground zero. I told him he was in a wonderful place and explained that no amount of risk could make his life any worse financially than it was in that moment. He had hit rock bottom, and it was up to him to decide if he wanted to lay there in the dirt or bounce back up to where he was before . . . or higher. Most people in that position would see only the limitations. I was trying to get him to see his situation as an opportunity.

I asked, "Robert, what would you do if you could do anything?"

"I'd buy real estate," he answered.

"Great. You don't even need any money to buy real estate!" I replied. He asked what I meant, and I said, "You can use other people's money to buy it depending on the type of deal you want to do. What specifically would you want to buy?"

Robert lived near Raleigh, North Carolina, and he'd been eyeing a $2 million piece of property along the river. An old, rundown mill sat on the land that had gone unused for many years since the textile business largely left America in the late 1980s and 1990s. He said, "I'd buy this property, demolish the mill, and sell the bricks, lumber, and copper. Then I'd either keep the land for myself or parcel it out and sell part of it."

"That's a solid plan," I said. "Why don't you do it?"

He looked at me like I was insane. "Uh, because I'm bankrupt and don't have any money laying around, much less $2 million or even enough to put a down payment on it."

Robert was still seeing only the limitations, not the opportunity. He came up to the limit and stopped—until I challenged him to push through to find the opportunity.

I asked him how long the property had been for sale and how much he thought he could get for the lumber, bricks, and copper. He said it had been vacant for years, and he was sure he could get at least $700,000 and possibly up to $2 million for the materials—which would essentially pay for the land and the building. He just didn't know how to get from where he was to where he wanted to be.

I said, "Okay, here's what you're going to do. The property has been on the market for several years, and now we're in a recession. Nobody is going to buy it, especially for $2 million. So, you're going to offer them $500,000 for it. Tell them it's an all-cash deal with no contingencies, but you'll need ninety days to close. Do that and then come back to me."

Robert did as I suggested and was surprised when the seller accepted his offer. Robert showed up at my office a week later to tell me the news. He also reminded me that he did not have any cash on hand, meaning he needed to come up with half a million dollars in ninety days.

"No problem. Now, get estimates for the bricks, lumber, and copper."

Robert went off and got the estimates, and then he reported back to me. The copper guy offered him $600,000, the lumber guy offered $800,000, and the brick guy offered him $1 per brick for the gorgeous nineteenth-century bricks on the old mill. I told him to accept all three offers and ask the buyers for a one-third down payment on the deal. Those down payments provided the $500,000 he needed to close on the property, which he actually bought outright at ninety days with the cash he got from the down payment on the materials. After the deal closed, the lumber, brick, and copper guys all came in and extracted the materials and paid Robert the remaining two-thirds they contracted for. At the end of the day, Robert owned the large piece of riverfront property outright and pocketed another $1.6 million on the sale of the materials. Over the course of ninety days, Robert went from bankruptcy and hopeless to a $1.5 million payday and twelve acres of paid-for North Carolina real estate along a river. More importantly, he learned how to see opportunities instead of just the limitations.

Once Robert learned this valuable lesson, he was off to the races. He repeated this deal about thirty times over the past decade, and today he's a multi-multimillionaire. Robert owns hundreds of acres and millions of square feet of industrial space, and he has an enormous net worth in properties and cash flow.

How did this happen? There's only one reason: Robert learned how to take an honest evaluation of where he was and where he wanted to be. He stopped lying to himself and fully owned his situation. He pushed back on the fear that had overwhelmed him in bankruptcy. He set good expectations. He stopped dreaming about *someday* and set daily goals for today. He focused his mind and took advantage of the people and resources that came alongside him to accomplish his goal. It is a perfect example of everything I've talked about—and I couldn't be prouder of Robert.

I tell this story all the time because I want people to believe that *they* can do the same thing Robert did. It's not magic or luck; it's the natural result of applying these success principles to your financial pie. Robert grew his pie exponentially over the course of a few months. Wherever you are, whatever your current situation may be, you can do the same thing. If you want to grow your financial pie, you've got to learn to see beyond the confines of the pie pan!

CHAPTER 6

Bridging the Gaps

*P*eople who hate their job are wasting their lives.

In my years as an advisor, I can't tell you how much time I've spent around people who are unhappy in their work life. They become deflated as they even speak about what they do for eight to ten hours a day. They complain about their businesses. They whine about their managers. They are concerned about how little impact they make or how unappreciated they feel. They are unhappy about *everything*. They often say they make a great living, but at what cost? Sometimes I'm amazed these people even manage to get out of bed in the mornings. Everything about them screams one painful fact to me: they've traded a piece of their soul for their income, and that's always a bad deal. Frankly, it's sad to watch.

Even worse, people do this in other parts of their lives as well. They complain about not having the right information, training, or experience to accomplish their goals. They stress about not having enough time to do the things they want or need to do. They rationalize how their financial struggles are someone else's fault. These things are like potholes that can bring your financial journey to a screeching halt.

After working with thousands of people professionally and through pro bono financial counseling sessions, I've found that most people are struggling to cross what I see as gaps in their life. These four areas—vocation, education, time, and attitude—may seem unrelated, but their combined impact on your success cannot be overestimated. If you want to protect and grow your financial pie, you've got to fill these four holes.

THE VOCATION GAP

I'd estimate that around 80 percent of the employees and about 40 percent of the entrepreneurs I've worked with are in a job or career that gives them only limited satisfaction. For an entrepreneurial guy like me, that makes zero sense. From a pragmatic perspective, you've got to think that the one thing we can control is our own lives—and that includes where we work. I hear people talk about how much they hate their jobs and think, *Well, why don't you leave? Why don't you start your own business? Why don't you find a way to monetize the things you actually enjoy?*

When you follow your passions, fulfillment follows; quite often, success is not far behind. It's easier for people to complain about their lives than to put in the effort of making a change, but the cost is severe. Their lives are slipping away like sand through an hourglass, and they're never getting that time back. I just want to grab these people by the shoulders and scream, "Stop wasting your life on things you aren't passionate about! If you hate what you do, get out and get out now!"

If you are more of a traditional workplace thinker, leaving a "safe" job to start your own business probably sounds insane. Jumping ship—even if the ship is sailing in a direction you don't want to go—can be terrifying. First, you lose the "security" of a traditional nine-to-five job. But what is job security? The Great Recession of 2008–2009 and certainly the COVID-19 pandemic showed us that there is no real security in any job. That sounds scary, but I think it is actually quite freeing. It gives you permission to picture a life outside of the "safe" confines of a job you hate.

Second—and this is the bigger deal for most people, even though they won't admit it—leaving a traditional job and striking out on your own means you'd lose the ability to blame someone else for being miserable at work. That may sound harsh, but I've talked to plenty of people who *need* to be able to point the finger at someone else. If you were to go off on your own, your success, failure, happiness, and frustration would all fall on you. In fact, the National Association for the Self-Employed reports that solo entrepreneurs working alone with no other employees account for 79.1 percent of all small businesses in the United States.[5] Some people just don't want that much responsibility. What they don't realize, though, is that they *already* have the responsibility for their own success and well-being. Even if you have a steady income, you're still on your own to some degree. There is no cavalry riding to your rescue, whether you have a nine-to-five job or not.

Look at it this way: In order to keep your job, you have to make the business a lot of money. Your efforts have to not only cover what you get paid but cover all of your support. Think of office leases, administrative help, insurance, all the other employees, and so on. The rule of thumb is that you need to generate three times your salary in revenue for your firm to keep you in your job. Does that sound like job security? When you look at it that way, it seems like we're *all* self-employed.

Even if you don't start your own business, simply moving from one job to another can be intimidating enough. We can get stuck somewhere between "the grass is always greener" and "the devil you know." We may *want* to leave, but we can feel trapped, bound to a job we hate by little golden handcuffs forged out of paychecks, deferred compensation, and benefits. What are we supposed to do when we hate our jobs but are scared to risk trying something new?

Take a breath. This isn't something you have to figure out today, but if you're in this situation, it's something you need to *start* figuring out. Life is too short to dread getting up every day. There aren't enough weekends to make up for a miserable Monday–Friday existence. Sure, you can stay and keep collecting those paychecks, but what's the point if you hate your life? What are you even working for if not for the opportunity to improve and enrich your life in ways that really matter?

Whenever I find myself in this type of rut, I always try to imagine what my future self would say to me today. I imagine ninety-year-old Erik Weir sitting in a rocking chair looking back on his life. What would he regret more: playing it a little *too* safe or not taking more risks and not having as much fun? I think most people regret the chances they *didn't* take far more than the ones they did. People avoid risk because they fear failure. The irony is that the only thing you can count on by avoiding risk *is* failure—failure to succeed at the life you really want.

What Is Your Job Costing You?

If you find yourself dreading Mondays, I challenge you to do a simple exercise: take stock of what your job is *paying* you versus what it's *costing* you. You can measure this in two ways: in terms of money and in terms of life satisfaction. Financially, I like to take a business approach. Most companies look at profit in terms of *accounting* profits and *economic* profits. Your accounting profit is the money you actually make. It's your income, or what you pay taxes on. Your economic profit is your current income in relation to your potential income. For example, you might love real estate and be capable of making $100,000 a year easily as a residential real estate agent. However, you're too scared to leave your $50,000 job as an account manager at a widget factory to risk starting a new career in real estate. In this case, you're actually taking a $50,000 *loss* in economic profit, because you're making $50,000 less than you could be making if you changed careers.

As for life satisfaction, I want you to take an honest, critical look at all the good things and all the bad things related to your job. Does it pay you a salary? What does that salary enable you to do? Does it offer remote working and freedom of location? Do you have good friends in the office you enjoy interacting with? Does your work bring help and value to others' lives? Is your work in line with your passions, interests, and aptitudes? Do you end your day tired because you know you did a good job or do you start your day tired because you know the work ahead doesn't really matter to anyone? Work through these and any other questions you can think of and write your answers down. The goal here is to consider every possible benefit and every possible detriment of your current professional situation.

Next, think about all the good and all the bad that could come with making a job change, whether it's moving to a different company or starting your own thing. Would the hours be better? Would you have more freedom to take time off or work from home? What would you want your new boss to be like, and how's that different from what you have right now? What are the people at the other business saying about *their* jobs? What would it look like for you to take a big swing and start your own business? Where would your clients or customers come from? How much could you earn? Would it be worth it to take a pay cut in order to have more satisfaction in your day-to-day life? Would you be able to enjoy your work more, travel more, spend more time with your family, donate more of your time to serving others, and other things that make life worth living?

Now, I'm not one of those guys who will tell you to go quit your job and "follow your passion" whenever you get frustrated. The fact is, I think a lot of people are in perfectly fine jobs, but they are unfulfilled in other areas of their lives, so they take it out on their employers. That's why I think it's so important to first take stock. You may find that the pros of your work far outweigh the cons.

I always try to imagine life as a wheel with spokes the way we have talked about in chapter 1. Vocation is only one spoke, but since it's where we spend the majority of our time during our working years, our work life tends to spill over into other areas. As a result, you may value a job that you can mentally and emotionally leave behind at the office at the end of the day, freeing you up to focus 100 percent on your family, relationships, and personal interests. That can be hard to do when you're running your own business or you're personally responsible for all the business outcomes. I'm a huge family guy, but I am also thinking about my work much of the time. It's at least rattling around in the back of my mind while I'm doing other things. I have to compartmentalize the different parts of my life to focus on one thing at a time, whether it's my kids, wife, work, studying for a test, and so on. But compartmentalizing often wears us out if we're not careful.

People are tired all the time because they spend so much time moving from one mental compartment to another all day long. When they're home, they're thinking about work. When they're at work, they're thinking about home. They struggle to stay present mentally—in the right place at the right time—and this causes fatigue and guilt. Zig Ziglar said, "No wonder you look tired. You're always traveling. When you're at home, you're thinking about work. When you're at work, you're thinking about home."

It might be difficult for you to completely unplug your brain from business. If so, then being able to "leave work at work" is probably a huge perk—maybe one you've never even considered. Regardless of your wiring, trying to live in the moment, with an eye for the future, has great benefits. Sometimes the little things in life turn out to be the big things, and the seemingly big things turn out to be the little things. It's important to be *focused* but also *present*. Life is a balancing act, and, as with any balancing act, sometimes a plate wobbles or falls. Live with grace, forgive yourself and others, and keep pressing on.

After taking stock of the costs and benefits of your job, you may surprise yourself and discover that your situation isn't that bad after all. It's not perfect (nothing is), but you are coming to appreciate what your job allows you to do, both at work and in other parts of your life. This is a legitimate answer; it's not a cop-out. You've wrestled through a major question, and now you can put it to rest. Let it go for a while, focus on the value you identified for your job, and enjoy it for what it is. This is a great way to live. Gratitude is a powerful motivator, and being truly grateful for the value your job provides can be a game-changer.

Since you've now willfully and intentionally made the decision to stay where you are for a while, train yourself to adopt a more positive attitude. Cut out the complaints and gossip. These things are simply exhausting and do nothing but destabilize the very foundation you're standing on. Instead, compliment the organization for what it does right. I'm not suggesting you "fake it till you make it"; I'm just suggesting you try to find a *real* happy face for a while. If you find yourself continually frustrated and unhappy later, you can always repeat this exercise, and maybe then it'll be time to leave.

What Would You Do If You Knew You Couldn't Fail?

Of course, you might take stock and realize without a doubt that it's time to make a change, and that can bring about a weird mixture of excitement and fear. This is where I suggest imagining a magic wand that wipes away all fear of failure. There's no way to ensure you won't fail in a job change or starting your own business, but you need to start by *pretending* there is no possible way to fail. This is what frees you up to dream. So, what would you do if you weren't afraid of failing? What would you dream if failure were impossible? This gives you a mindset that sets you up to win.

Too often we allow ourselves to paint a bleak picture of our own future failures. It's easy to consider leaving a good-paying job and think, *I'm giving up a steady paycheck. I'm taking too big a risk. If this doesn't work, I'll go bankrupt. I won't be able to buy food for my family. Our cars will be repossessed. We'll lose our home. Our lives will be ruined.* Some of us are more prone to these little mental death spirals than others, but we've all been there a time or two. But here's the thing: the outcome we fear the most almost never happens. Yes, it's possible that you make this big change, try to start your own business, and it doesn't work out. You might fail. What will that mean *really*? We live in a nation of safety nets. Welfare, government assistance, food banks, bankruptcy laws, and charities are in place to help catch us when we stumble and fall. It's not ideal, and I know you don't *want* to rely on them, but that's why they're there. You aren't really stuck out on a limb all alone. Try to push past your fear of fatal failure and dare to dream about the professional life you could build for yourself.

When I was a kid, I watched my parents' cars and even our washer and dryer get repossessed. It was obviously alarming, but it was also quite calming somehow. My parents couldn't make the payments, so they lost some of their stuff. That's it. No one came to the house and beat them up. No one judged us. The "repo man" even apologized as he hauled our things away. In the process, our family downsized—or *rightsized*—our budget, we moved in with family members for a little while, and my parents rented out our home to avoid losing that too. In one fell swoop, everything we feared happened . . . and it wasn't that bad. The fear of *what if* was swept away, and Mom and Dad began to climb out of the hole we were in. Less than a year later, Dad moved us across the country, founded a company, and then sold it for more money than he'd ever made in a year! Life under a dark cloud is depressing only if there's no hope for sunny days ahead. There's something about hitting rock bottom that is encouraging: there's nowhere to go but up!

My goal here isn't to get you to stay in a job you hate or to launch your own new enterprise. All I'm trying to do is give you some context for evaluating a possible vocational gap between where you are and where you want to be. Your job isn't everything, but it is the source of most people's income and livelihood. If you want to keep or make a big, round, delicious financial pie, you've got to be intentional about creating a working lifestyle that is rewarding, enjoyable, and sustainable. If yours isn't, it's time for an evaluation (if not a change).

THE EDUCATIONAL GAP

If you don't continue to learn and grow, you are actively losing value every year. You aren't just standing still; you're moving backward. Education is power in the marketplace of ideas. The minute you stop learning is the minute you start losing value in the marketplace. The best telegram operator or fax machine technician in the world is practically worthless today. Why? Because the world has moved on, and those who don't move with it by keeping their skills sharp and/or learning new skills will be left behind. They'll fall into what I call *the education gap*. They confuse time on the job or seniority with worth!

Better Yourself, Not Just Your Paycheck

As I write this book, I'm fifty-four years old, the owner of multiple businesses, and a multimillionaire who's made more than $1 million in personal income every year for the last twenty-five years. I'm also a student, working toward a master's degree at Harvard. I am an extremely busy guy, so you may be wondering why I'm carving time out of my schedule to power through a master's program at one of the world's toughest schools. It's simple: there are some things I don't know that I want to learn. Even at this stage in my life, I identified an educational gap that I felt was keeping me from being the best version of me possible.

The funny thing is, this degree won't do one thing to make me more profitable. It won't make any impact whatsoever on my personal income. In fact, I will likely earn a bit less for a while due to the time I spend studying. But isn't the potential for higher income the reason people usually continue their education? They want to qualify for the next big promotion or make themselves more valuable in the marketplace, so they add new letters behind their name. We all know doctors, lawyers, CEOs, CFOs, COOs, CPAs, nurses, pastors, and teachers who have pushed themselves through *just one more* degree to reach the next rung on their industry's pay ladder, and there is absolutely nothing wrong with that. I am a big believer in education; I just don't think people should put themselves through all that simply to make a few extra bucks a year. I'd much rather have people advance their education to better *themselves*, not just better their paycheck.

Learning in the Digital Age

There has never been a better time in the history of the world to be a lifetime learner. It's trite to say that the internet has changed the world. What's sometimes not noticed as much is that the internet has revolutionized learning. My children will never know the frustration of having a question they couldn't answer with just a few taps on a phone screen. Any question, random piece of trivia, or calculation can be solved in seconds. My seven-year-old has more powerful technology in his pocket than what was used to put the first man on the moon when I was his age!

Education—not just information—has also changed dramatically over the past twenty years. You can now earn advanced degrees from prestigious universities without ever stepping foot on campus. Most of my Harvard program, in fact, is online. The fact that I'm nearly one thousand miles away from Harvard's campus doesn't affect my studies at all. That was unthinkable just twenty-five years ago. Online learning has exploded in that time, with resources like Khan Academy, Skillshare, Lynda.com, and Chegg revolutionizing how people learn. Even YouTube can be an excellent teacher on virtually any topic, with everything from TED Talks to videos on how to fix a leaky toilet freely available 24/7.

During the COVID-19 pandemic in 2020, schools across the country were forced to shut down in-person instruction for months. Teachers, students, and (of course) parents were unexpectedly thrust into the world of online learning, using video conferencing and e-learning tools from kindergarten to college. Some kids thrived whereas others struggled. The long-term ramifications of our collective crash-course in online learning will no doubt be studied for years. But let's get real. How big an impact do you think all these changes to education will make on your financial pie today? My guess: none. If you really want to grow your pie and make yourself more valuable, I suggest you look at the methods of the past at least as much as you look toward the future.

The Timeless Power of Mentorship

For literally thousands of years, craftsmen have taken apprentices under their wings to teach them a trade and show them the ropes, from the masons of ancient Egypt to the blacksmiths and shoe cobblers of medieval Europe to the carpenters of the Middle East. We still see the power of apprenticeship today in medical doctors' residency programs, during which these well-educated men and women get real-world training under more experienced doctors. Most of us, though, will experience this kind of professional tutelage as simple mentoring, which has become, I believe, the best-kept success secret in the world.

I cannot oversell the importance of mentorship in the modern world. No matter how available basic information is today, no matter how accessible formal education has become, nothing beats working alongside an expert for a period of time, always asking him or her questions about what they've learned, how they've navigated their career, what pitfalls they've fallen into, and what wisdom they've gained over many years. I've had many, many mentors throughout my life, going all the way back to my teens when I shadowed my mother to learn the ins and outs of real estate.

After hiring many people for my businesses over the past thirty years, I've learned that a basic college degree doesn't go very far in the real world. If you give me someone right out of college who had a perfect GPA but had no internships, they're usually no help to me at all. But a B or C student who had three or four internships with different companies and leaders throughout their college years? Those young men and women are gold. They're infinitely more valuable on day one than the academic who did nothing but study.

So if you're in college, look for internships in your chosen field. It shouldn't be hard; everyone loves free labor! If you're out of school already, I still suggest going after internships and mentorship opportunities as if a grade depended on it. If there's someone you really want to learn from, approach them and offer your time and service for free. I've been on the giving *and* receiving end of this type of relationship, and my life is richer for it. Sometimes, just getting twenty minutes with someone you respect can make a huge difference in your life and career.

Back in the days before Uber and Lyft, eager learners would offer to drive guest speakers to the airport just to have a half hour of one-on-one time with them. I did that myself a time or two. This can be precious time that pays huge dividends in your life. You will be surprised just how many people will give you twenty minutes if you just ask, come prepared, ask good questions, and take lots of notes. Always be on the lookout for opportunities and send a thank-you card when someone gives you some of their time. Almost everyone loves sharing with someone who is eager to learn.

If you do get someone's ear, whether it's for a one-time, thirty-minute chat or a long-term internship, be sure to follow my four-step plan for maximizing your time together:

1. **Ask Questions.** Plan ahead by preparing questions in advance. Write them on a scrap of paper or in your phone's "Notes" app. Then, whenever you find yourself with some one-on-one time with your mentor—even if it's just a few minutes—pull out your list and pepper them with questions.

2. **Shut Up.** Remember, you're there to learn from this person. That happens only when you stop talking and focus on listening to what your mentor has to say. Back-and-forth conversations are great, but if you're talking more than one-third of the time, you're talking too much. Shut up and listen! Remember, we have two ears and one mouth for a reason.

3. **Take Notes.** Don't trust your memory; it will let you down. A short pencil is better than a long memory! Your mentor will share insights with you that will affect your business for decades to come. You're not going to remember every word off the top of your head. I suggest you either take notes during your conversations or at least try to write down everything you remember as soon after your meetings as possible.

Even better, ask permission to record your conversations so you can go back to them, outline them fully, digest them, and use previous discussions to inform your future conversations with your mentor.

4. **Keep It Brief.** Your mentor's time will always be more valuable than your own, so make the most of whatever time they give you. I recommend never asking for more than twenty minutes. Any longer than that, and you'll probably never get a meeting. Also, make it easy for the person to say yes. Offer to meet at their office or wherever is convenient for them. If you ask for a twenty-minute meeting but make them drive to a coffee shop to meet you, you're really asking for an hour or more of their day.

The successful men and women you see as potential mentors today were once young and in need of advice as well, and they relied on the time and generous help of others just like you do now. People are often hesitant to ask a more successful leader for their time, but I've found that potential mentors love telling their stories and find fulfillment in helping others. And if you take their advice and make positive change, they will most likely give you more time because they'll see you're serious about improving yourself and learning from them. If you only listen and never do what they say, they'll see you for what you are: a waste of their time. They'll move on and find someone who *really* wants their help.

Even today, I regularly seek mentorship from people further along than I am. There's always room to improve, and there's always someone who can teach you how to do something and how *not* to do something. This is the best, most proven, and most invaluable way I know to bridge an education gap. I have learned from people from all walks of life, including billionaire corporate leaders, political figures, and even an Uber driver who blew my mind. You can find gold anywhere if you keep your eyes open.

THE TIME GAP

Your time is valuable. No, I mean it is *really* valuable. Every hour of your day has a monetary value. This is something professionals like attorneys and CPAs, who bill their time by the hour, are acutely aware of. The rest of us seem to forget it though. That's why we allow ourselves to "lose time" throughout the day like it's no big deal. We might even laugh it off, saying something like, "Well, the day got away from me." But this isn't funny. Every hour that slips through your fingers is taking dollars right along with it.

Think your time management isn't stealing your pie? Think again. In his great time-management book *Free to Focus*, productivity whiz Michael Hyatt reports that the typical office worker loses at least three hours a day to basic interruptions. The time cost of those interruptions is staggering, causing employees to lose 750 or more hours every year to simple interruptions and distractions that could have been avoided with even minimal effort.[6] If we're talking about a forty-hour workweek, that's almost nineteen weeks of time that could be spent on key projects. Nineteen weeks! How much more effective and productive could you be if you recovered those lost nineteen weeks of productivity?

It's not just about productivity though. That lost time has a dollar cost. Let's say you make $100,000 per year and assume there are two thousand work hours per year (fifty weeks at forty hours per week). That means your time at work is worth $50 per hour. Multiply that by the 750 hours you might be losing to unnecessary interruptions, and we're talking about $37,500 in lost value. If you're in sales, that could be much more in lost commissions every year! That kind of waste adds up. I don't know about you, but I don't want 40 percent of my financial pie going out the window to mindless time wasters and interruptions.

So, how does that happen? Think about lunch, for example. The clock strikes noon, and you get up from your desk, walk over to the deli across the street, wait in line for twenty-five minutes, buy a $12 salad, sit down and eat it, and then stroll back to your office. If I were to ask most people what they paid for that lunch, they'd say $12. Wrong. The actual cost of that salad was $62—the $12 they paid for it plus the $50 in lost time they spent getting it themselves.

Instead, imagine your officemate is breaking for lunch and heading out for a salad. You could say, "Hey, I'll buy your lunch if you bring me a salad back." That person agrees, and you have a salad delivered less than an hour later that you can eat at your desk. Your out-of-pocket cost is now $24 (for two salads), but you *made* $50 in that hour because you stayed focused on what you were doing. That one little change took you from losing $62 (your time plus the cost of your salad) to earning $26 ($50 minus the cost of two salads). That's an $88 positive change in position from this one decision on one day. Do that every day for a year, and you've created $22,000 in value!

This is just one quick example of how to pick up marginal utility. You could apply that same lens to things like spending an hour a week in a grocery store versus ordering groceries online or cleaning your house versus hiring a housekeeper a few times a month. You can also start tracking how much time (and value) you're throwing away on things like social media, reading texts and emails the instant they arrive, drop-in visits, unnecessary meetings, water cooler discussions about last night's football game, and all the other little things that steal our time like an endless stream of pickpockets. You have only so much time, and you need to pay attention to what wasting it is costing you.

The impact of workplace time wasters is especially apparent to people who begin working from home or who become self-employed after spending years in a traditional office setting. For example, a friend of mine spent the first twenty years of his career working in typical nine-to-five offices before leaving to start his own solopreneur venture at forty-three. Prior to leaving, he was a VP in a $100-million organization and led a team of more than thirty people. This was a busy guy who was used to getting to work early, staying late, and answering texts and emails well into the nights and weekends.

He spent anywhere from two to six hours a day in meetings most days and constantly had a stream of people coming in and out of his office. After working like this for so long, his first month working for himself left him feeling . . . off-balance. He set goals for each day just as he'd always done, but he was shocked to cross the last item off his list by noon every day. How was this possible? Then it dawned on him: he'd eliminated nearly every distraction and, for the first time in his career, was able to spend his time laser focused on his task list without phone calls, meetings, emails, and drop-in conversations getting in his way. He was far more productive in far less time, and he was able to make conscious decisions about how to use his newfound wealth of time. With more and more people leaving the office and working from home, the secret is getting out: the standard office environment can be a black hole of time wasters.

Now, is it okay to "waste" a little time here and there in the name of fun and leisure? Absolutely. It's *not* a "waste of time"; it's an investment in yourself and your family. Living a balanced life means making time for relaxation, and taking time off helps us enjoy life and brings us back to work more focused and energized. We can even get an unexpected energy boost before a planned vacation because we're looking forward to it so much. It's like sprinting the last hundred yards toward a finish line. So I'm not saying you should never "waste" any time; I'm just saying you should know when and why you're doing it. Choosing how to spend your time should be as intentional as choosing how to spend your money. If you want to do something, do it! But as with your money, just be clear on whether you're making an investment, taking a reasonable expense, or simply throwing your time away.

THE ATTITUDE GAP

Over the past thirty years I've been honored to help literally thousands of people with their money. Much of that work has been pro bono in partnership with my church. In that kind of setting, I have more latitude to go beyond the facts, figures, and spreadsheets most people associate with financial counseling and dig deeper into the heart matters behind people's financial issues. You see, most people think money is all about math. It's not. More often than not, a money problem is just a symptom of a bigger internal problem. To fix the money problem, we have to first root out the underlying emotional issues.

A Bitter Pill

As I dig into these things with people in financial crisis, I always ask about their upbringing and their relationships with their parents. Practically every one of them has nothing but bad things to say about one or both parents. I have been shocked at the level of bitterness, resentment, and outright anger middle-aged men and women have expressed to me about their parents. These people have been carrying this pain around for thirty, forty, or fifty years, and it feels just as raw and powerful today as it must have been when they were kids. And now, as adults, these people are expressing that hurt through self-destructive money habits. The bitterness they've carried around for most of their lives has created a seemingly uncrossable chasm between where they are and where they want to be financially.

Bitterness has been described as a poison you prepare for someone else and then drink yourself. It slowly eats away at your spirit, robbing you of joy, poisoning your relationships, and standing in the way of your goals. It spreads like cancer through entire families as relationships become uncomfortable and awkward, which only compound your feelings of isolation and depression.

I'm sure you've seen the effects that bitterness and resentment have on people. We've all known people who simply never look happy. They had a rough childhood. Someone did something to them they can't get over. An injustice was done against them, and everyone else in their life pays the price. These people are quick to be offended, defensive, suspicious, angry, and are altogether unhappy. They blame others for their shortcomings, lash out at the people closest to them, and genuinely have no idea how harsh they've become with others.

They're so consumed with bitterness that their hearts have turned to stone and they instinctively erect walls around their lives to protect them from more pain. People with this kind of stony heart have a hard time giving or receiving any kind of love.

This is such a sad thing to see, and yet I've seen it in nearly every person I've counseled through financial crisis. When someone's driven by such extreme levels of bitterness, it shouldn't be a surprise that their pain affects every area of their lives and is manifested in poor money decisions. Money is often used as a bandage to help mask or temporarily alleviate pain. It's a more socially acceptable form of escapism. People may get concerned if we drink too much, but those same people will likely cheer us on if we medicate our pain by buying a new car or an expensive toy. But both are ultimately harmful, self-destructive behaviors.

Bitterness Is a Poor Motivator

When I was in fifth grade, my favorite teacher was Mrs. Beaneert. I often stuck around after class to help her clean up just so I could chat with her for a few minutes. Often a male teacher would walk in to see her too. This guy was a total jerk to me. He made fun of me and my stutter relentlessly. He'd always walk in and say, "Hey Stutters, I see you're sucking up to the teacher again, huh?" One day he even said, "Wow, Stutters, you're going to be a great wife one day." I was humiliated. And furious. I dreamed of getting back at him for treating me like this.

By age eighteen, I'd earned my black belt in martial arts and had become a competitive fighter. I'm embarrassed to say that I used to dream about running into this guy so I could show him what I thought about how he treated me. When I was twenty-eight, I couldn't take it anymore, and I called him out of the blue. I told him who I was, I explained that I had dreamed of beating him up for twenty years, and I told him that I used my memory of him as my motivation in my fighting matches. I'm not sure what I thought would happen; I just knew I couldn't carry all that bitterness for one more day.

This man, now in his late forties or early fifties, almost started crying. He felt so bad about how he'd treated me, and he begged me to forgive him. He explained that he had a crush on that other teacher himself, and he was just trying to get rid of me every afternoon so he could have some one-on-one time with her too. I felt such a huge weight come off my shoulders as we spoke and as he expressed his sincere grief over what he'd done to me. It dawned on me how much of a prisoner I'd become to my bitterness, how much time I'd wasted focusing on the pain he had caused me so long ago. For the first time in twenty years, I felt free. The crazy thing is, I could have felt like this a long time ago, but I chose to carry my bitterness with me instead of forgiving him and moving on. I thought my bitterness made me stronger. I thought it gave me an edge in my fighting. I was wrong. All it did was make me miserable—for no good reason.

I don't think I'm the only one who has tried bitterness as a motivator for success. Instead of setting a goal to become a millionaire for their own financial security and happiness, for example, some may do it as a way of getting back at the person who hurt them. A recently divorced single mother might think, *He never thought I could achieve anything on my own, but I'll show him!* A young professional might think, *Dad has never been proud of me, but he'll be forced to admit how talented I am once I get this promotion.* The more we've been hurt, the more we're driven to prove ourselves to the one who hurt us. This attitude is deceptive. It makes us think we're being proactive when we're really just letting our pain drag us around by the nose. And it almost never ends the way we want. I know people who spent their entire careers working to gain someone else's respect, only to be disappointed when it didn't happen. I've seen this drama play out often enough to know that when bitterness and resentment are your driving forces, you're never going to get the affirmation you're looking for.

It may be hard to believe, but the people who hurt you may not even *know* they hurt you. You might have spent years focused on the pain while they remain oblivious. And someone who doesn't realize they've harmed you will never understand the distance you've allowed to grow between you. They may be just as hurt by your bitterness-driven response as you are about whatever they unknowingly did to you!

Overcoming Resentment

Overcoming a lifetime of resentment is no easy task, and it's certainly beyond the scope of this book. However, I can share a few tips based on my work with many people who have been forced to confront the poisonous effects of bitterness.

Step 1: Look for the Blessings

I always suggest people start by adopting an attitude of gratitude. Simply put: be thankful. Everything you have experienced, every relationship, every job, every high, and every low has brought you to where you are. Sure, it's probably not all good, but there's at least *some* good. Call out the blessings in your life. Find the good in it. You can always find a blessing in any situation if you train yourself to look for it. No, I'm not saying you should put on a fake happy face and smile through your pain. I'm not that naive, and I know some people have been through excruciating experiences I couldn't even imagine. However, I've never met a person who couldn't find *something* to be thankful for. Learning to look for those things, even under a pile of hardships and heartbreaks, changes how we view everything else in our life. So, keep short accounts of offenses and long accounts of things to be grateful for. That's the key to changing your thinking.

Step 2: Learn from the Pain

As much as we want to say we learn the most on the mountaintop, it's not true. We learn the most in hardship, when the path is unclear and our future uncertain. Don't run from the fear, pain, and tears. Embrace it, grow from it, and move on. Even in your darkest hour, when you think you'll never smile or laugh or love again, you will. Just as surely as the sun sets, it will rise again.

Step 3: Help Other People

The problem with bitterness is that it keeps our attention on ourselves—our pain, our hurts, the wrong that was done to us. Serving others lifts our eyes and enables us to see the needs of other people. Sometimes the best thing you can do when you're buried under a pile of bitterness and self-pity is to get out of your comfort zone and find a way to help someone who's much less fortunate than you are. Without fail, every time I serve food at a soup kitchen or help a local nonprofit, I have one or two conversations that change my life in some way. Not too long ago, I was sorting clothes for a local shelter and struck up a half dozen different conversations with other volunteers, people who worked there, and the underprivileged clientele of the charity. In those settings, I always keep my business success to myself, because I don't want people to be distracted. I'd rather hear about *them*. I want to hear their stories and benefit from the lessons they've learned. Of course, I love helping people with my time and resources, but I'm not foolish enough to think I'm only there to *give*. What I get out of those situations is always worth much more to me than what I put in.

Giving our time, money, and energy gives us the chance to make a positive change in someone else's life, which in turn lifts our spirits and gives us a sense of purpose and fulfillment like nothing else. We need other people. We were created for community, and nothing grows community like working *for* and *with* other people.

Step 4: Look for the Lesson

Whenever you're faced with a bitter disappointment, betrayal, or loss, try to ask yourself, *What can I learn from this?* Is there something you could have done to avoid this loss? Is there a lesson you could apply to your future efforts? How might today's disappointment prepare you to win tomorrow?

This is especially difficult when we're dealing with betrayal. Nothing hurts more than being hurt by someone we love. I once heard someone say, "Sometimes the person you'd take a bullet for is the one standing behind the trigger." That is, the people we love the most are often the ones who hurt us the most. Why? Because our love gives them power—power to lift us up . . . and power to destroy us. Being vulnerable with someone is difficult, and having that vulnerability betrayed blows a hole right through us, destroying trust and breaking relationships we thought would last forever.

If you're in such a situation right now, my encouragement is to find a way to forgive that person and, if desired, restore the relationship. No, they may not *deserve* your forgiveness, but grace is never earned; it can only be given. Relational breaks that stir up bitterness carry within them the potential for miraculous restoration. The lessons we learn about ourselves and others during times of pain are often the most powerful, life-changing lessons we'll ever learn. Don't waste them.

Step 5: Forgive

Walking around with a heart full of bitterness is like running a race while wearing a backpack full of bricks. At some point, in order to finally run free, you must choose to take that backpack off. That means granting forgiveness—or at least having a hard talk with the offending party to clear the air. Even if the offender has long since passed away and you can't speak to them, still set yourself free by forgiving them. Otherwise, your bitterness will continue to weigh you down, taking all your joy with it.

Contrary to popular belief, forgiveness in this sense isn't an entirely selfless act. You don't forgive the other person because they've asked for or deserve it; you forgive because it's the best thing for *you*. Imagine redirecting all the anger, bitterness, and resentment toward problem-solving and strategic thinking, which results in wealth creation. Picture yourself regaining all the time, energy, and passion you've invested in your bitterness and reinvesting it into ideas and actions that will improve your life, work, and money. You are planting seeds with every action you take, and those seeds will return whatever is planted. If you sow bitterness, you'll reap more bitterness. If you sow forgiveness, you'll reap forgiveness. If you sow joy and opportunity, you'll reap those things as well. With every action, you are choosing what you're sowing and what you'll eventually reap. If you're planting bad seeds today, don't complain about the bad harvest you'll reap later. Even if you've been hurt deeply by someone, you still have a choice about what you'll plant and harvest.

CROSSING BRIDGES

The things we've discussed in this chapter—vocation, education, time management, and attitude—may seem like a mixed bag of random topics. To be honest, I could probably write an entire book on each of these areas; they are *that* important to your long-term financial success.

Obviously, my goal here wasn't to provide an exhaustive commentary on each topic but rather to introduce these four things as powerful factors in your financial life that you can't afford to ignore. Whether you're struggling to fill a void in your job, education, time, or attitude (or all the above), let me encourage you that you *can* bridge the gap. All it takes is time and focus. Remember, I'm in my fifties and at the height of my career, but even I dragged myself back to school to fill some knowledge gaps at this point in my life. You can do the same. And there's no deadline; you've got enough time to cross these bridges, but you don't have time to waste. If you've been putting off dealing with a gaping hole in these or any other areas, it's time to get to work. The safety and sweetness of your financial pie depend on it!

CHAPTER 7

The Power of Clarity and Planning

My boys like to read Harry Potter books. In the first book, there's a great scene where Harry has to choose his first magic wand. He goes through several that obviously aren't a fit before the shopkeeper takes a risk and hands him a very special wand. And *boom*. It's magic. Everything comes together, and Harry literally *feels* the magic coursing through him.

In the real world, there's no magic shop that will help us find the perfect wand. We have to make our own. No, I'm not talking about wizards and spells; the magic wand I'm talking about is the mindset that erases all limitations and shuts down all self-limiting thoughts. It's the ability to champion an idea, taking it out of the clouds and forcing it into reality no matter what obstacles stand in our way. That kind of idea—that *vision*—is what excites people. It's what draws people alongside us to help. It's what makes people, partners, resources, money, time, and talent appear out of nowhere.

It's like magic.

Of course, once I wave my magic wand and get the ball rolling, I know I'm going to have to step out of the fantasy and deal with some real-world issues. My magic wand doesn't *really* remove all limitations; it just enables me to see through them. When you wave your magic wand, you put yourself in a mindset where you allow yourself to *believe* that you can attain or accomplish anything. You *believe* you can have financial independence. You *believe* you really can drive that dream car you drool over every time you see one at a red light. You *believe* you really can have the kind of marriage you always dreamed of. Your magic wand shows you that anything is possible. I love looking at possibilities with my magic wand—but I never stop there. If you stop with the dream, all you've done is made a wish. But there is no fairy godmother who's going to fly down and make your wishes come true. You have to do that for yourself.

To really take yourself, your relationships, and your finances from where you are right now to where you want to be, you have to back up that "magic-wand thinking" with some real-world planning, clarity, and activity. And you do that by setting goals.

MAKE YOUR GOALS SMART

Most goal-setting frameworks refer to—if not outright steal—the longtime favorite *SMART Goals* paradigm. I've seen this in dozens of productivity books and articles, so I won't dwell too much on it here. However, because it is "the old standard" when it comes to setting goals, it's certainly worth at least a passing mention. The SMART model originated in a 1981 paper written by George Doran. Though different writers have plugged in different words for the SMART acronym, Doran originally listed five criteria, teaching that SMART goals must be

- **Specific:** clearly state a desired outcome
- **Measurable:** include quantifiable progress markers
- **Assignable:** specify who will do the work

- **Realistic:** be based in reality, no matter how unlikely that reality may seem
- **Time-related:** have a deadline for completion[7]

Focusing on these five areas brings much-needed focus and specificity to your goals and holds you accountable for what you want to accomplish and when you will do it. It's a great recipe for writing your goals, making sure your written goal statements cover all the bases.

For example, let's say you're in sales making six figures, it's the first of the year, and you want to buy that Tesla, which we'll price at $80,000. Instead of saying, "I want to buy a Tesla someday," let's turn it into a SMART goal. You could write, "I am going to buy a current-year, long-range Tesla Model S with cash for $80,000 in January of next year. To do this, I will generate $6,500 per month in new sales commissions to dedicate to my car fund." This makes things much more concrete, doesn't it? It's *specific* because you've said exactly which model you want and how much it costs. It's *measurable* because you know how much you need in savings total ($80,000), and you know how that breaks down per month in new sales commissions. It's *assignable*, of course, because you're doing the work yourself. It's *realistic* because you're already making six figures, so you clearly know how to sell. And it's *time-related* because you've put a clear deadline on when you plan on making the purchase. Congratulations, you've checked all the boxes! Now all you have to do is get to work!

Personally, I like to take this a step or two further. If this were me, I'd visit the nearest Tesla showroom or delivery location. I'd sit in the car, breathe in the brand-new vegan leather interior, run my hand over the pristine dashboard, and grip the steering wheel in a solid "ten and two" position. I'd imagine myself launching from a stoplight, going from zero to sixty in two seconds. I'd have someone take a picture of me sitting in the driver's seat. When I got home, I'd put that picture somewhere I'll see it several times a day—on my bathroom mirror, my desk, or even make it my computer wallpaper.

I'd go out of my way to keep my goal in front of me in a real, tangible way to continually feed my motivation as I work toward my goal.

Then, I'd get to work accomplishing my goal using the system I'll outline in this chapter—but with one addition. I'd make a list every day of the top five or ten things that are standing in between me and my dream, and I'd attack those things starting with the biggest, scariest, hairiest, most intimidating item on the list. Once I knock that obstacle out of the way, I'd move on to the next, continually clearing my path. This little secret can speed up your success exponentially.

Smarter Goals

I like the SMART goals model, but I don't think it's perfect. It's often rightly criticized for failing to accommodate long-term goals, especially in how to break down big goals into smaller, monthly/weekly/daily pieces. That daily grind is what turns enormous, world-changing goals into your everyday reality. So, I want to spend most of this chapter discussing how to build goal-based routines into your daily life. Whenever I'm making big goals, especially things that will take a while to accomplish, I always do these three things:

1. Start with the end in sight
2. Build backward
3. Set many milestones

Let me break this down a bit.

Start with the End in Sight

Epitaphs tell the story of your life. It's like a story I heard about a grieving woman standing over her husband's grave. Upon reading the headstone, which read, "Loyal husband, loving father, and best friend to all who knew him," the woman burst into uncontrollable sobbing. The pastor conducting the service said, "Oh, dear woman. I'm so sorry for your loss. He will surely be missed."

"It's not that!" she cried. "I just read the epitaph and realized I must be at the wrong funeral!"

Don't leave your epitaph to chance; write it yourself. Look decades into the future and decide today what you want to be remembered for. Then, live your life to *be that person*. That's what I mean by starting with the end in sight. You want to look all the way to the end of the road to see who you want to become and what you want to have accomplished with your life. Only then can you start to figure out how to actually accomplish all those things in the time you have and leave the world a better place.

I encourage you to do this with your life in general, and I want you to do it with each one of your goals. You don't need a crystal ball; just determine at the outset what the desired end result looks like if there were no limitations, if you had access to all the capital, resources, intellect, skills, talents, and people you needed to accomplish your goal. This is your magic wand. It really helps to dream without restriction since great dreams build wings of talent, influence, and connection. It's the idea that changes the world!

Build Backward

Once you know where you're going, start building backward from the finish line. Instead of trying to guess which steps *might* lead you where you want to go, imagine yourself already having accomplished the goal, then work your way back to the start. Say you want to own your own business five years from now. Picture yourself in that future and look back. What relationships got you there? What training was required to qualify you for that level of leadership? How much capital or money was required? How much sweat equity or time was required? Where did it come from? Who was indispensable on the journey? How did you meet that person? Remember, the process is the reward and the joy; arriving at the destination is just the cherry on top.

Set Milestones

A massive goal is rarely a single goal. Rather, it's the result of accomplishing many, many smaller goals. Whatever your big goals are, the best way to reach them is to break them down into smaller, more manageable, more achievable chunks. One day, all you might do is give your initiative a name. That's a win! When you break big goals into smaller pieces, you're setting yourself up for regular wins throughout the project, and all those little wins propel you forward.

I'm sure plenty of people want to become a millionaire someday, but precious few people have turned that wish into an actual goal. And even fewer have turned that goal into a *real* goal, complete with long-, mid-, and short-term milestones. In the Tesla example, we knew the finish line was $80,000 cash in the bank by January. Working backward from that goal, we were able to break it down into monthly milestones, or subgoals, of $6,500 per month. Saving $6,500 feels much more manageable than coming up with $80,000 to most people. But what happens if you "fail" and save *only* an extra $4,500 per month? All that means is that it'll take you eighteen months instead of twelve to save up $80,000. Sure, it'll take you six months longer, but you'll still be driving a new Tesla at the end of it. Is that really a failure? I don't think so.

Or, if your goal is to run a marathon in six months, you could sign up for a series of shorter races between now and then. You might run a 5K in a month, then a 10K the month after that, and work your way up to a half marathon within three months. At that point—three months into your six-month time frame—you're halfway to your goal. Those subgoals aren't just building stamina; they're building confidence. They're showing you that you really can do this, even if running twenty-six miles once seemed impossible. Every little victory proves to you that you are capable of achieving the enormous goals you've set for yourself—as long as you put most of your focus on the little goal ahead. Success builds on success, so be sure to plan for all those little successes on the journey. You can do this!

MANAGING YOUR GOALS

There are plenty of books that talk about how to automate your goals, put your goals on autopilot, and accomplish your goals with minimal effort. That is *not* this plan. Again, goals are not wishes. A wish is something you make once and then hope for the best. A goal, however, requires constant management. You refuse to go to bed until you have made progress, and you drive ahead daily even if it's a tiny step. Forward momentum is key, and setbacks won't stop you from pressing ahead.

That's not to say you should be a slave to your goals. It's just the opposite, in fact. You're the boss. You are in charge of your goals—creating them, refining them, working toward them, accomplishing them, or failing at them. It's all up to you. When I talk about managing your goals, then, I mean you need to devote time every day to make sure your goals are working for you and that you are doing the right daily activities to ultimately accomplish your big goals. I believe few things in life are sadder than wasted time. Time is pretty much the only resource we can't get any more of. Once it's gone, it's gone. That's why rich busy people buy airplanes; they are literally time machines. The time they save not having to deal with airports, TSA, and traffic is literally worth millions to them.

You may not be ready to buy a jet, but let's see what else you can do to make the most of the time you have each day.

Step 1: Make Time Every Night

Every night—literally seven days a week—I spend up to an hour working on my goals. At this point in my life and as busy as I am, that fact shocks most people. I've had CEOs and entrepreneurs turn their noses up at me and reply, "Up to an hour? Are you crazy? I can't do that. You may have enough free time for that, but I can't afford to waste that much time every day." Most of the time, it's not that these people don't have time to spare; the problem is that they're spending the time they have poorly.

I've had a few friends get gastric bypass surgery. You know what I noticed? They all lost weight. That's because they changed the size of their stomach. Even if they wanted to eat more food, they physically couldn't. It turns out that being forced to limit food intake really does make people lose weight. I wish we could come up with some kind of gastric bypass procedure for time management. People waste so much time every day, but they still want more. If they'd put hard limits on their entertainment and distractions—their *intake*—they'd be amazed at how much fat they'd lose from their day.

When people tell me they're too busy to spend time every night planning the next day, what I hear them saying is, "I'm too busy to spend time becoming more productive!" Even worse, there's an insult in this reaction as well. They're really saying they can't believe *I'm* willing to waste *my* time working on my goals. They're basically patting me on my head as they completely write off the method I and others have used to generate trillions of dollars in wealth, save countless marriages, land man on the moon, and cure diseases. If you don't want to spend time working on your goals every day like I do, that's fine. But don't tell me it's a waste of my time. Every success I've ever had has been filtered through this process. It just works. If you plan, you will be ahead of 99.9 percent of everyone else, regardless of any other limitation.

The time I spend working on my goals each night—anywhere from twenty minutes to an hour—is literally the most high-value portion of my day. Nothing else I do all day comes close to matching the wealth-creating impact of my nightly goal-setting routine. This has been proven countless times throughout my career. It's such a fundamental belief for me that I can barely comprehend when someone tells me they "don't have time" to work on their daily goals. I think, *You don't have time to do the most important thing you could be doing? Then all you're doing is wasting your time!*

Setting aside this time every night is easy—if you make it a priority. How much time do you spend after dinner watching TV, zoning out while Netflix's autoplay feature keeps you entertained for hours? How much time do you spend scrolling through social media feeds? Would you consider those to be high-value activities? There's nothing wrong with watching a show at night to relax, but you can't let four hours of binge-watching tonight steal tomorrow's productivity. Whatever you're doing at night, I'm almost certain you can find at least twenty or thirty minutes to plan the next day. It doesn't even have to be the last thing you do at night. In fact, you could make this the last thing you do at work every evening before you leave for the day. Block out the last thirty minutes of day for a meeting *with yourself*. Treat it as you would a meeting with your boss or your largest client. Take the time seriously, and don't skip it!

But what will you do with this time you're carving out? How exactly can thirty minutes of planning tonight make you ten times more effective tomorrow, literally saving hours of wasted, aimless time? Easy. If you do what I suggest every night, you'll start every day of your life knowing exactly what you need to accomplish to make progress toward your goals. You'll literally be solving your biggest problems all day, every day—even when you're focused on other things—because you'll be directing your entire day toward your success. So, the first step of the process is to make time for the goal-setting ritual below. Try to carve out forty-five minutes to an hour at first. Once you get used to the process, you'll grow much more efficient with this time and will probably get it down to around twenty minutes per night. I usually do nights so my mind is clear and all my random thoughts about my next day's tasks and plans have been addressed. When I'm done, I sleep great. If morning works for you, go for it. It's not the time of day as much as just doing it regularly.

With this new pocket of time you've created (notice I said *created*, not *found*), grab a pencil and a notebook, your laptop, or even just your phone and Notes app, and spend your time doing the two activities below. Use whatever format works for you. I still use a pencil and paper, as there is something about writing it down by hand that engages me a bit deeper than notes on my phone or tablet.

Step 2: Identify Your Biggest Problem and Solutions

Once I'm alone in my dedicated time to work on my goals, I always start by asking myself, *What is the biggest problem I need to solve?* This could be anything. Sometimes my biggest problem is a challenge

I'm having with a business deal. Sometimes it's a relationship issue. Sometimes it's an exam or a paper I have due for my master's degree. Sometimes it's securing funds for a piece of property I want to buy. Sometimes it's a fitness challenge. Whatever it is, I write it at the top of a piece of paper like this: *The biggest problem or challenge I'm facing right now is (fill in the blank).*

Now, why would I start this time every night by focusing on my biggest problem? Wouldn't that be demotivating? Well, yeah, it probably would be . . . if I stopped there. But here's the deal: most days, I'm *already* thinking about my biggest problem anyway. You probably are too. We can't help it. When we're worried about something, it tends to consume most of our mental capacity. Trying not to think about our biggest problem at any given minute is about as effective as trying not to think about pink elephants. Once it's out there, your brain is off to the races. Since you're probably already thinking about your biggest problem anyway, why don't we make those thoughts more productive?

Once I have my biggest problem articulated and written at the top of the page, I challenge myself to come up with twenty potential solutions for that problem. That's a lot of solutions. Honestly, I often can't come up with that many, but I always use twenty as my target to really stretch myself. Besides, you'd be surprised how often number eighteen turns out to be the right solution! Trying to come up with this many solutions forces me out of a problem mindset and into a solution mindset.

There's no time or energy left for wallowing and whining because I'm actively working on solving the problem. And when I look at my sheet of paper, what do I see? I see only one problem but twenty different ways to solve it. My solution-to-problem ratio is 20:1! That isn't depressing; it's life giving! It's a constant reminder that there is *never* a problem without at least a handful of solutions. In more than thirty years, I've never been unable to write down at least five potential solutions to any problem. Think about how different you will feel with five potential solutions.

You can also use part of this time to research other people who have faced and solved a similar problem, whether that's through online research, scanning through books, or talking to mentors. In my experience, there's rarely a problem I'm facing that someone else (probably someone I know) hasn't already solved. If so, I want to know how they did it. Of course, I may not copy their solution, but it can at least give me a starting place for charting my own course through the issue. For example, I think about all the people who tried to climb hazardous mountains like Mount Ararat. Many tried and failed before Friedrich Parrot and Khachatur Abovian made their historic ascent in 1829. These two were the first, but they certainly weren't the last. As others took up the challenge, they rightly examined which route Parrot and Abovian took. Even if future explorers choose a different route, simply knowing what worked for their predecessors enabled them to make better, more informed decisions. The same is true in business, money, relationships, and every other part of life. If you know how someone else solved a problem you're currently facing, you can examine what worked for them and see how you might apply all or part of their solution yourself.

Once I have a good list of possible solutions, I rewrite the list in priority order. That is, I make the best, most likely option number one, the next most likely solution is number two, and so on. And, to be fair, a list of twenty possible solutions will no doubt have some stinkers. That's OK. The goal isn't to figure out twenty things that *will* work; the goal is to identify twenty things that *might* work. It takes only one good solution to solve a problem. When you start with twenty options, there's a good chance at least one of them will work.

Now that you have a list of potential solutions to your biggest problem, let's turn that into an action plan for the next day.

Step 3: Plan Your ABC Goals

Every morning when I wake up, I know exactly what I need to do that day. My time is valuable—far too valuable to leave to chance. And guess what? So is yours. Like I said before, time is the one resource that isn't, under any circumstances, renewable. Everyone, no matter who they are, where they are, or how rich they are, gets twenty-four hours a day. The difference between the super successful and those who are struggling comes down to what each one does during those twenty-four hours.

I know that's a strong statement, but I'll double down on it. If you aren't intentional about how you spend your time each day, you will never be successful. Period. How do you expect to manage monetary wealth if you can't even manage time, the one resource you get absolutely free and in the same amount as everyone else? If you get out of bed each morning with only a fuzzy understanding of what you need to do to advance your goals, you aren't going to make it. You may luck into a win every now and then, but there will be no ongoing, steady growth.

It blows my mind that people think it's okay to coast through their days. What do they think is going to happen? Do they expect someone to knock on the front door with a bucket full of answered prayers and realized dreams? That's not going to happen. In fact, you should expect just the opposite. *Someone* is going to decide how you spend your time each day. If you don't decide, then you're just handing the reins of your life off to your boss, your coworkers, your team members, your spouse, your creditors, your competitors, and even your enemies. You're letting everyone else manage your most precious resource. Again, you wouldn't do that with your money, so why on earth are you doing it with your time?

But this is how most people live, isn't it? They get to work with a very general idea of the day's priorities, but the day goes off-track by 9:00 a.m. the first time an unexpected visitor appears in their office door. They let one person distract them onto another task, then it happens again and again. They respond to every email and text message as they arrive, drilling holes in the day like a block of Swiss cheese. They attend meetings that don't really require their presence. They disappear for lunch for an hour and a half because they "need a break." They get roped into other people's drama. They make a dozen trips to the coffee pot or water cooler. In the blink of an eye, it's 5:00 p.m., and they haven't done a single protective thing to advance their own interests. Instead, they've been dragged around by the nose all day by other people, used as a tool to help others accomplish *their* goals. These are the people who get home exhausted every evening yet have no idea what they did all day. Why should they? They didn't have a plan for the day, so they didn't know what they were going to do anyway. And as the saying goes, those who fail to plan actually plan to fail. Failure is the *only* thing you can count on when you start a day with no road map for where you want to be before nightfall. Sounds harsh, but it's true.

That's why I never start the day without a plan—and I'm not talking about my calendar. Yes, my calendar shows me where I'm supposed to be and when, but my calendar isn't in charge of me. My calendar is simply a tool to empower my work toward my goals. Don't fool yourself into thinking your calendar and your goals are in sync. For most people, they're miles apart.

But you can change that, and here's how.

I practice what's generally known as *ABC Goal Setting*. This is a popular technique that I've heard from many speakers and authors, but the guy who really sold me on it is the great motivational speaker Brian Tracy. I picked this method up from Tracy decades ago, and I combined it with my nightly routine of identifying my biggest problem and twenty solutions. Now, once I finish that exercise, I use my problem/solution list to write out my top fifteen activities for the coming day using the ABC method.

First, I look at my problem/solution list and my calendar and ask myself, *What are my most critical tasks for tomorrow?* By critical, I mean what is on my plate that is both important and urgent. Those two words—*important* and *urgent*—tell you exactly what deserves (or demands) your attention each day. We are generally good at identifying what's *important* (even though we often don't act on it), but we're terrible at understanding what's *urgent*. Urgent reflects the activity's place in time. If something is urgent, it has to be handled

ASAP. But—and this is key—just because something is urgent doesn't mean it's important. An email from a coworker asking your opinion on something isn't important, but it can feel urgent, especially if the coworker puts a little pressure on you to respond. In that case, the issue may be important to your friend, but it isn't to you. However, we often take on the importance it has to someone else. We allow their activity to trump our own and, in doing so, we're admitting that our coworker's time is more valuable than ours. Why else would we allow *their* important issue to skip to the head of the line of things we're supposed to be doing ourselves?

Success depends on your ability to say no to things that don't move the needle on your goals. Sure, you can and should help other people whenever you can, but you can't let everyone else's goals take priority over yours. You are responsible for *your own* success—no one else's. Help when you can, but don't neglect your own goals.

So, thinking about everything you *could* do in a day, I want you to identify what is truly important (to you!) and what is truly urgent (to you!). Be ruthless here. If something is important but doesn't have to be done immediately, it doesn't belong on this list. There will be a place for it later. That could be a sales report that is due to your boss in two weeks. Yes, it's important because your job could depend on it. But it's not urgent—yet. It will graduate to your critical list soon enough.

OK, now you're going to write the letter *A* next to the things that are both important and urgent. I personally aim for five items. After all, if I strike off five important and urgent tasks each day, I'm doing far better than the average person who's being dragged along through the day by an endless string of distractions. I'd bet the majority of people go home at night without completing even *one* of these items most days, but I set my sights on *five*!

Once I'm looking at five A-level tasks, I prioritize them 1–5. So A-1 is the most important, most urgent thing I need to do the next day. If I don't do anything else, I need to make sure I get A-1 done. Once I'm done with A-1 (and only once I'm done with A-1), I'll move on to A-2. Then A-3 and so on. That gives me my top five high-priority items for the day.

Next, I look over the list of things I *might* do tomorrow and ask, *What is important but not urgent?* These are B-level tasks, so I write the letter *B* next to them. Again, these are things that need to get done, but I have a little time before they become urgent. Any work I do on my B-level list simply saves me time and trouble later, when those items become urgent, and anything that isn't addressed at the B level eventually "graduates" to A level as it becomes more urgent. This is where you park things like the sales report that's due in two weeks. I identify the top five B-level items for the day, prioritize them as B-1, B-2, and so on, and list them under my five A-level items. Now, if I'm incredibly efficient the next day, I know exactly what ten things I can accomplish.

But what about the things that aren't necessarily important or urgent? That's where my third and final list, the C-level items, comes in. There are always things we *could* do in a day that aren't really important or urgent, but we still want to do them. Playing golf for a couple of hours to blow off steam, watching the newest binge-worthy show on Netflix, or enjoying a novel are good examples. The only thing that's *wrong* with these activities is that they steal time from the higher-value activities on our A- and B-level lists. I still want to account for these things, though, so I make a third list of C-level items that are neither important nor urgent but would simply be nice to do.

These are things like washing my car, picking up or dropping off dry cleaning, ordering a book I don't plan on reading for a few months, reviewing a new car purchase, studying a white paper on Bitcoin, or planning a ski trip or summer trip. They are sort of nice-to-do activities but are neither important nor urgent. I pick the top five of these activities, prioritize them starting with C-1, and stick them at the bottom of my list. Eventually, some of these will work their way to B- or even A-list items. After all, if you're a residential real estate agent and have a showing scheduled in the afternoon, you need a clean car to make a good first impression.

At this point, I have fifteen items on my to-do list for the next day: five A-level items, five B-level items, and five C-level items. With that, I end my nightly goal-setting time and usually head to bed, knowing that I'll be focused and prepared to attack the day from the moment I wake up. The weird thing, though, is that doing this right before bed changes how I sleep. It's like I'm programming my brain to keep problem-solving while I'm asleep. I can't tell you how many times I've woken up at 2:00 a.m. with the answer to what I identified that night as my biggest problem. And it's not that uncommon for me to wake up so energized and excited for the day that I end up knocking out my A-1 and A-2 items before breakfast! These action items don't necessarily require a lot of time; they usually just require *intentionality*. When you're intentional about what you need to accomplish and what problems you need to solve, you'll be shocked at how quickly and easily the answers tend to present themselves.

Three Final Warnings

Let me close this breakdown on my process with three quick warnings. First, if it hasn't become apparent yet, you need to write these lists down. Do not trust yourself to keep up with them in your mind. You will fail, just like I've failed every time I've tried to keep up with my task list without writing it down. When we write it on paper or on a screen, we are making a commitment that *these* are the things we know we should be doing. It's a contract we're making with ourselves, and it's a contract you need to put in writing.

Second, do not expect to cross out all fifteen items on your task list. In the thirty years I've been doing this, there hasn't been a single day when I've made it all the way to the bottom of the list. In fact, most days I never get past A-5. That's okay! We fill the list to make sure we always know what's next, so it's always better to have more to do than we can ever accomplish in a day. That's why we prioritize the list from most important and most urgent to least important and urgent.

In fact, there are many days when my A-1 item takes the whole day. When that happens, I'm not worried about the other fourteen things on my list, because I know I'm moving my business forward by focusing on the single most important thing I have to do. An A-1 phone call in the morning can change the entire direction of my business and open up new opportunities I never expected. When that happens, I embrace it, even if I can't get to any other items on my list for the day. Sometimes the first item on your list has more of an impact on your success than the other fourteen items combined!

Then, each night when you sit down for your goal-setting routine, you'll have that day's incomplete list of tasks to refer to. Use that along with your problem/solution exercise and your calendar to plan the next day. Carry over any incomplete tasks from one day to another as needed, but don't assume you *have* to keep them on your list. View each day independently. There will no doubt be some A- or B-level items on your list one day that simply disappear the next.

Third, if an item on your task list requires someone else's input or a meeting with several stakeholders, do not fall into the corporate assumption that a formal meeting has to be at least thirty minutes in length. Too often we schedule meetings for a half-hour by default, but guess what? Your calendar can set meetings for however long (or short) you want! Some of the most successful, most productive businesspeople I know have the default meeting time on their calendar application set to ten minutes. I've personally planned and managed multimillion-dollar deals in ten-minute chunks. If you know you'll need more time, then by all means plan for it. But don't assume you need thirty minutes when ten will do.

THE POWER OF FOCUS

In my experience, there are only two things that can truly limit your progress: the *messages* you fill your mind with and the *people* you spend your time with. Or as the great motivational speaker Charlie "Tremendous" Jones put it, "Five years from now, you will be the same person you are today except for the books you read and the people you meet." By reading this book, you're choosing to put something new in your mind. That's great! But it won't change anything if you don't take the next step by putting action behind this information. You do that with goals.

I'll say it again: the time I spend each night reviewing my goals and setting my action plan for the following day is the most high-value twenty to sixty minutes of my day. Everything I have accomplished or will accomplish is the result of the time I've spent planning. This level of planning keeps you focused, and when you're focused—truly focused—on a goal, you can do anything. There's a quickness in your step. You can do more in forty-five minutes than most people do all day. I am convinced that I routinely accomplish three or four days' worth of work in a single day compared to most people. And it's not because I'm smarter or somehow special; it's simply because I'm focused on my plan. I don't waste time, because I know exactly what I'm doing now, what I'm doing next, and what problem I'm trying to solve. I try to minimize my interaction with people who waste my time so I can get massive tasks accomplished quickly.

This emphasis on focus and planning is nothing new. I certainly didn't create it, and neither did Brian Tracy, Franklin Covey, Zig Ziglar, or any of the other productivity and motivational experts I've learned from. Abe Lincoln famously said, "If I only had an hour to chop down a tree, I would spend the first forty-five minutes sharpening my axe." A centuries-old proverb states, "Measure twice, cut once." Everyone from Mark Twain to Blaise Pascal has been attributed with saying, "If I had more time, I would have written a shorter letter." Church reformer Martin Luther said of one particularly busy day, "I have so much to do that I shall spend the first three hours in prayer." All of these are age-old testimonies to the power of planning. Time spent in focused thought (and prayer, if you're a person of faith) *bends time*. It seems counterintuitive, but more time spent planning usually enables you to accomplish more things in less time. It maximizes efficiency and demolishes limitations that would otherwise stop you in your tracks.

I'm a firm believer that success depends on your ability to focus intensely on one thing until that thing is done. I call this the *touch it once* philosophy: point all your cannons at the task in front of you and keep firing until it's dust. Do not stop until the job is done. Then, point those cannons at the next thing and start firing again. This kind of focus, planning, and intentionality is essentially a super-power these days. Most people can't do what I'm describing. Instead, they focus on something for a little while, get distracted or bored, and then shift their focus onto something else before the first thing is finished. As a result, they end up with a dozen different partially finished tasks and projects. Everything is open or in progress, and nothing is complete. That's a terrible way to live.

If your financial success is a pie, then your goals are the crust that's holding everything together. If you want a bigger pie, you need to make a bigger crust. I challenge you to "grow your crust." Don't be like everyone else. Put in the time to make your days ten times more productive. Identify your biggest problem and a list of solutions. Prioritize each day's goal-focused tasks using the ABC method. Then start the day focused on your A-1 task, and don't move on to A-2 until the first one is finished. If you need a break, try to save it for when you're between tasks instead of interrupting your flow halfway through one. If you realize your daily goals are too massive to accomplish in a day, spend your planning time that night breaking your tasks down into smaller pieces—a discipline called *chunking* activities.

The idea is that your daily actions need to be small enough to touch once and complete before moving on to something else. If you can't accomplish one task on your list without taking a few breaks or suffering several distractions, your action item "chunks" are too big. Break them down into smaller pieces. You need the motivating rush of crossing goals off a list as you work through the day. Having a single giant goal sitting open on your list for months at a time is a horrible demotivator, so if you realize you haven't broken your big goals into small enough tasks, make that today's big problem to solve and revisit your goal sheets. This is *your* world, and you get to make the rules. If something isn't working, keep tweaking it until it does!

And no matter what, keep moving forward! An inch of progress is still progress! But if you've put in the time and effort of setting goals and planning your day, you'll almost certainly move much more than an inch at a time. A good friend of mine is a member of the Navy SEALs—one of the country's most elite fighting forces. He explained that 90 percent of a SEAL's job is just showing up. Then, their training and preparation takes over and gets the job done. Your success, much like a Navy SEAL, will depend almost exclusively on your preparation. Life will absolutely give you unprecedented opportunities, so be prepared to make the most of them. Life is short, so live with vigor and intentionality!

ACTIVATING
FINANCIAL
SUCCESS

CHAPTER 8

Income Growth and Management

Most people are working for someone else. They're putting in forty hours a week at a nine-to-five office (or maybe start earlier if they are working in a trade like construction), have a livable salary with regular paychecks, may or may not have a 401(k) plan at work, and have settled into a financial routine. They probably have some credit card debt. They're worried about the kids' college. They get a 2–5 percent salary increase every year or can pick up overtime when needed. They're putting *something* aside for retirement, but they aren't sure it's enough, or worse yet, they *are* sure it's *not* enough. They aren't rich, but they're getting by. I call this group *wage earners*.

Then there are the people who are self-employed, maybe working by themselves or with a few other team members. This could be something like a creative professional, business consultant, financial advisor, insurance salesperson, or a tradesman. These people have irregular incomes, meaning there is no biweekly paycheck that's set in stone. It can feel like feast or famine for these men and women, and there's no guarantee what their income could look like next week, next month, or next year. Their income could double in a year, or it could dry up completely. It's a risk, but it's a risk they like taking. For some, it's all they know. I call this group *entrepreneurs*. Even though they don't control their income, their effort has a more direct (or at least more immediate) correlation to income. They often feel they can get an edge, and if they can, they can experience growth.

Neither group is better than the other, and the world needs both. If you're a wage-minded person, I'm not going to try to convince you to start your own business. If you're an entrepreneur, I'm not going to try to convince you to go to work for someone else. However, as we talk about the next slice of your financial pie—income growth and management—I do need to address each group separately. There are some options, opportunities, and risks that are associated with each type of worker, and I want you to have a clear plan of action regardless of what you do for a living.

One note before we get into this: I'm only telling you what has worked for me personally or what I have been able to glean from talking to thousands of people over the years. Every individual's situation is a little different and needs specific attention. For that reason, I suggest you use what I'm going to lay out here as a guide for your discussions with your financial advisor. This is *your* money we're talking about, and you need to take an active role in managing it. That means working with a professional who can walk you through the ins and outs of each option and financial product so you can be confident in your decisions. Never follow a financial advisor's advice blindly, including mine. Get in the weeds, get your hands dirty, and learn what you need to know to manage your money.

It's really not that difficult, but it can be overwhelming at first. Think about the first time you tried to ride a bike or drive a car. It may feel second nature today, but it certainly didn't the first time you tried. Ultimately, the more time you spend learning about and working with investments, the more comfortable you'll be during both the highs and lows of the market. Plus, we now have access to tools that as recently as twenty years ago were available only to professionals. This easy access to financial tools, education, and information means our comfort with investing and income management is only getting better.

INCOME MANAGEMENT FOR WAGE EARNERS

If you're working a traditional job, your level of income is largely dependent on others. Sure, you can get raises by making yourself more valuable, but there's only so much you can do to substantially increase your paycheck. The key for you, then, will be what you do with the money you make. Specifically, there are six steps you can take to make sure you're maximizing your income and building wealth for the future:

1. Save for emergencies.
2. Take advantage of your employer's 401(k) match if one is available.
3. Pay off your credit cards.
4. Invest in 401(k)s, Roth 401(k)s, and IRAs.
5. Utilize indexes and growth mutual funds.
6. Invest in real estate mutual funds or physical real estate.
7. Save for your children's college with 529 plans.

I'll cover each one of these in detail, but first we need to address the biggest issue, the one thing that will enable you to work through each step with gusto, a concept I call *save the raise*.

Save the Raise

As a salaried employee or wage earner, you most likely get pay raises every year. It may not be much, but you should at least be getting standard cost-of-living increases even if you aren't getting performance-based raises and/or bonuses. If so, the single most important piece of advice I can give you—the thing that will make an immediate, exponential impact on your wealth building—is to save the raise. That is, develop the discipline to maintain a level standard of living and devote any pay raise, bonus, and "found money" to your long-term wealth building.

For example, let's say you have a job making $50,000. After your first year, your boss gives you a customary 5 percent raise, bringing you up to $52,500. Here's what I want you to do: forget the raise. You've lived on $50,000 for a year at that point; the truth is, another $2,500 (or $208 per month before taxes) won't change your life that dramatically. Yet plenty of people act like they hit the jackpot when they get a raise like this. How many people do you know have gotten a $200/month raise and used it as an excuse to get a new $400/month car payment? That leaves them $200 *worse off* every month. Who wants to get a raise and end up with *less* money? What a waste!

Instead, I suggest you put that extra $2,500 into your retirement accounts, which we'll discuss. The next year, you get another raise to $55,000. Great! Now, you're putting $5,000 extra toward wealth building. Another year, another raise, and you're putting $7,500 extra toward retirement. Pretty soon, you're putting $10,000, $15,000, or $20,000 into your retirement accounts and seeing those balances start to rise. If you start this early enough, such as in your early twenties when you start your first job, you're setting yourself up for massive wealth much faster than you could imagine—especially if you're married and you and your spouse are *both* saving your raises.

Let's do a little math. Assume you invest $2,500 a year at age twenty-five, and you add $2,500 a year to that amount until you max out at $25,000 a year. Now assume you maintain $25,000 a year until age sixty-five, and you earn an average annual return of 10 percent. What would that look like when you retire? Let's see . . .

Age	Beginning Balance	Investment	Interest	Total
25	-	2,500.00	250.00	2,750.00
26	2,750.00	5,000.00	775.00	8,525.00
27	8,525.00	7,500.00	1,602.50	17,627.50
28	17,627.50	10,000.00	2,762.75	30,390.25
29	30,390.25	12,500.00	4,289.03	47,179.28
30	47,179.28	15,000.00	6,217.93	68,397.20
31	68,397.20	17,500.00	8,589.72	94,486.92
32	94,486.92	20,000.00	11,448.69	125,935.62
33	125,935.62	22,500.00	14,843.56	163,279.18
34	163,279.18	25,000.00	18,827.92	207,107.09
35	207,107.09	25,000.00	23,210.71	255,317.80
36	255,317.80	25,000.00	28,031.78	308,349.58
37	308,349.58	25,000.00	33,334.96	366,684.54
38	366,684.54	25,000.00	39,168.45	430,853.00
39	430,853.00	25,000.00	45,585.30	501,438.30
40	501,438.30	25,000.00	52,643.83	579,082.13
41	579,082.13	25,000.00	60,408.21	664,490.34
42	664,490.34	25,000.00	68,949.03	758,439.37
43	758,439.37	25,000.00	78,343.94	861,783.31
44	861,783.31	25,000.00	88,678.33	975,461.64
45	975,461.64	25,000.00	100,046.16	1,100,507.80
46	1,100,507.80	25,000.00	112,550.78	1,238,058.58
47	1,238,058.58	25,000.00	126,305.86	1,389,364.44
48	1,389,364.44	25,000.00	141,436.44	1,555,800.89
49	1,555,800.89	25,000.00	158,080.09	1,738,880.98
50	1,738,880.98	25,000.00	176,388.10	1,940,269.07
51	1,940,269.07	25,000.00	196,526.91	2,161,795.98
52	2,161,795.98	25,000.00	218,679.60	2,405,475.58
53	2,405,475.58	25,000.00	243,047.56	2,673,523.14
54	2,673,523.14	25,000.00	269,852.31	2,968,375.45
55	2,968,375.45	25,000.00	299,337.55	3,292,713.00
56	3,292,713.00	25,000.00	331,771.30	3,649,484.30
57	3,649,484.30	25,000.00	367,448.43	4,041,932.73
58	4,041,932.73	25,000.00	406,693.27	4,473,626.00
59	4,473,626.00	25,000.00	449,862.60	4,948,488.60
60	4,948,488.60	25,000.00	497,348.86	5,470,837.46
61	5,470,837.46	25,000.00	549,583.75	6,045,421.20
62	6,045,421.20	25,000.00	607,042.12	6,677,463.32
63	6,677,463.32	25,000.00	670,246.33	7,372,709.66
64	7,372,709.66	25,000.00	739,770.97	8,137,480.62
65	8,137,480.62	25,000.00	816,248.06	**8,978,728.69**

You'd have just under $9 million with this strategy! That's a lot better than a "comfortable" retirement!

Of course, your lifestyle changes as you get older, and you may need to bring some of that raise home. I know plenty of single moms for whom an extra $200/month could mean the difference between life and death. If you really need to boost your monthly income with your pay raise, that's fine—but think differently about it. What if you used only 75 percent of the raise and put the remaining 25 percent toward wealth building? Or split it 60/40? Or 50/50? Every little bit you invest today makes a huge difference later. If you're twenty-five years old, every $100 you save today could be worth thousands—even more than $10,000—at retirement. That's the power of compound interest—a concept Einstein rightly called the eighth wonder of the world.

And if you don't think one or two percentage points of additional return makes a big difference, consider this. After forty years, a single $100 investment would grow to $2,500 at 8 percent interest. Not bad, right? However, if you got 12 percent interest instead of 8 percent, that same $100 over the same forty years wouldn't just grow to $2,500; it would be worth $12,500! So, the difference between 8 and 12 percent interest isn't *really* 4 percent. In this example, that "4 percent difference" is actually a 600 percent difference! And remember, this is a *single* $100 investment. Just imagine what could happen if you invested $100 or $500 or $1,000 every single month for forty years. You'd be loaded!

Are you going to get 12 percent on all your investments? Probably not—at least not in the more common investments like index funds and mutual funds (which we'll discuss later). But there are many, many investments that have produced at least a 12 percent rate of return for decades. It's really not as hard as you might think ... if you know how to look for opportunities.

Who wouldn't want to turn $100 into $12,000? With what you'd spend on a fancy steak dinner for two right now, you could take your spouse on a high-end, weeklong luxury vacation anywhere in the world to celebrate your retirement. It's hard to keep this in perspective, but every single dollar you can save goes a long way toward the lifestyle you can enjoy later in life. Wasting a dollar today costs you somewhere between $25 to $120 of potential dollars forty years from now. If you can get this, it will help you become a wise investor and a millionaire.

For this reason, I don't want you to stop at just saving your pay raises. I want you to build a habit of saving *any* "found money." For example, it's not uncommon for homeowners to get a few hundred dollars back as a refund from their mortgage escrow account every year. Maybe you bought a new washer/dryer set that came with a $100 mail-in rebate. Maybe your grandparents surprised you with a $1,000 gift out of the blue. Maybe you sell an old sofa at a garage sale, or you sell other things you don't need any longer on eBay or Craigslist. So often in these situations, our brains get a dopamine hit and we immediately start thinking of what we can buy with this unexpected cash. Don't do it! Develop a mindset that instinctively knows this isn't *spending* money; it's extra *investing* money!

If you start this early enough, the power of compound interest will kick in and you'll find yourself with tens or hundreds of thousands of dollars in savings before most of your friends even *start* to take their retirement plan seriously. That puts you in a position of financial stability, giving you the chance to lift your eyes out of the weeds of the day-to-day grind and start asking yourself, *What else can I do? Do I enjoy my job? Do I have the financial foundation to risk trying something else?* It also empowers you to advance quickly to the next level of wealth building, real estate investing, which we'll discuss later. That's when things can *really* take off.

Most money books suggest saving 10 percent of your income throughout your working life. That's a fine strategy. You can totally do that and build wealth. But I know you could also do much, much more. From a young age, I set a goal of living on half my income and saving/investing the other 50 percent. I know that sounds crazy, and I know it's not possible for many people and many incomes. But again, just think differently.

One of my wealthiest friends, for example, gives away 50 percent of his business profits every year and still grows his company so quickly that his profits have doubled every three years for the past few decades. His total earnings this year will end up being the same amount he'll *give away* in just three short years. For example, if he earns $100,000 total this year, in only three short years he would be earning $200,000 and giving away $100,000. He's done this for so long that he literally gives away billions of dollars every year. How is this possible? Because he thinks differently. He made philanthropy a priority early in his career, and he's aimed all his cannons at that goal. He's one of the wealthiest men in America today, but he drives an older car and lives in a modest home. He knows every dollar he saves is a dollar he can put to work—for himself and for others.

That kind of wealth and giving may seem out of reach for you right now. That's okay. If 10 percent is all you can do, then do it. You'll likely retire a millionaire. But if you can save 20, 30, or 40 percent of your income, you'll be at a completely different level of wealth. Of course, it will require some sacrifices along the way, and there will be days when you can't take your eyes off your buddy's fancy new sports car. But ultimately you'll get to the point where you can buy a *fleet* of cars with less stress than everyone else has about buying one.

Now, with that big issue out of the way, let's quickly run through the six steps that will lead an employee into long-term wealth building and financial security.

Step 1: Save for Emergencies

Life happens, and it usually costs us money. Cars break down, people get sick, houses need upkeep. When these things happen— and they will—you need some cash on hand to take care of them. Otherwise, you'll reach for the credit card or, worse, raid your investments to pay these unexpected bills.

Those with a secure job and steady paycheck, such as teachers, government employees, or people working for a large corporation, should aim for at least three months' worth of expenses in savings. Notice I'm not recommending three months of *income* but rather, three months of *expenses*. What does it cost you to live for three months should you have a disruption in your income? If you remember the 2008–2009 financial crisis, even government agencies furloughed employees and suspended pay temporarily. The employees were eventually paid for the furlough, but there was a disruption. You don't want to find yourself with no financial buffer in those times, since that is when very bad financial decisions are often made out of haste and desperation. Three months should be enough to cover most surprises and provide a comfortable buffer between you and "life."

Employees who have variable incomes, such as salespeople, retail employees, and restaurant servers, need to have more. These people have the same type of surprises as everyone else, but they have the added pressure of potentially having a dry spell if their income craters for several weeks or even months at a time. Just think of all the restaurant and hotel employees who suddenly found themselves completely out of luck when the COVID-19 shutdowns began. Restaurants were packed one day and completely empty the next. It took nearly a year before dine-in service was available again in many states. That's an extreme example, but it illustrates how those with fluctuating incomes can be the most vulnerable if they're caught without savings. For that reason, if you fall into this category, I suggest putting six months' worth of expenses into savings.

When I say savings here, I mean put this money in a basic savings or separate checking account. Don't get fancy with this money; it's for emergencies, *not* for investing. You need to be able to access this money quickly when the need arises. Keep it separate from your everyday checking account and forget about it until you need it. If you invest it, you're not only making it less accessible, you're also adding unnecessary risk to the money that's supposed to *protect* you from risk. If the economy takes the kind of hit that could endanger your job, you can be sure that's the exact time the market will go down as well. Then, you could be out of work and your savings could be cut in half at the same time. Bad move. This should be money set aside to protect you when things go south—so set it aside, keep your hands off it, and pray you never need it.

If or when you do need to use some of these funds, replace the money as quickly as possible so you always have a fully stocked emergency fund.

Step 2: Employer 401(k) Matching

One of the most exciting ways to build wealth is to use *someone else's* money to do it. We'll talk about a few ways to do that in the next chapter, but the first experience most people have using other people's money (OPM) is through a 401(k) plan with a company match. This is literally free money. It is an instant, guaranteed, 100 percent rate of return. You won't find that kind of deal anywhere else in the world of wealth building.

The 401(k) is simply a company-sponsored retirement plan that gives you the chance to invest pre-tax dollars into a selection of funds that your company's fund manager selected. By *pre-tax*, I mean your contributions come out of your gross pay before you pay any income tax. This is the most basic form of tax-deferred investing. That is, you don't pay any income tax on the money you *put in*, but you will pay taxes on the money you *take out* in retirement.

Here's why the 401(k) is marketed as a good deal. Say you have $100 to invest. If you pay income tax first and you're in a 25 percent tax bracket, you have only $75 left to invest after taxes. However, with the 401(k), you get to put that *entire* $100 into your retirement account, which gives you the benefit of the growth on that extra $25 that you would have paid in taxes all the way from now until retirement. So, you're effectively investing 25 percent more than you would have otherwise. The downside is that you'll pay a lot more in taxes later because the government will take the taxes out of the growth. That is, instead of taking $25 today, they'll take 25 percent (or whatever bracket you're in at retirement) of everything that $100 earns between now and then. It's like if you are a farmer and you are paying tax on the harvest and not on the seed. This makes the 401(k) a good deal for you but a *great* deal for the federal government later. It's kind of like the federal government has a savings account *inside* your savings account.

The 401(k) is a decent financial vehicle, but it's not the best. That's why I recommend you use the 401(k) *only* if your employer offers a match and only *up to* the match. The match is essentially an incentive to encourage you to invest, and it's a good one. If someone wants to give me an extra 3, 4, or 5 percent of my income in the form of a 401(k) match, I'm definitely taking it. Like I said, it's the only way I know to get a guaranteed 100 percent rate of return. Even if the funds in the 401(k) stay stagnant and have zero growth over the next twenty years, I'm still doubling my money because of the company match.

So if your company offers a match, take it. If they don't, then I suggest you skip the 401(k) entirely and move directly to a Roth IRA, which I'll discuss. And if your company offers a Roth 401(k) option with a match, that is definitely the way to go. A regular 401(k) offers tax-deferred investing, but a Roth makes it totally tax-free.

Step 3: Pay Off All Debt except Cars and Mortgages

Once you've got sufficient savings for emergencies and you're taking the match on your 401(k) (if available), the next step is to get out of debt. Now, I'm not one of those financial guys who is completely against all forms of debt. I actually think specific types of debt under certain circumstances can be a powerful tool in your wealth-building plan. But basic consumer credit card debt is *not* one of those circumstances. The average US household currently has a credit card balance of a little over $7,000.[8] Stop playing around with this type of wasteful consumer debt! If you're carrying a balance on your credit card, it's time to pay it off once and for all.

There are two good ways to pay off this debt. First, you could pay your cards off from smallest to largest by balance. This way, you can knock out the smallest debts quickly, build some confidence and momentum, and then push forward into the larger debts. Getting the little ones out of the way fast also frees up those old minimum payments, leaving you more to throw at the bigger debts. Alternatively, you could pay the debts off from highest to lowest interest rate. This technically saves you more money in the long run, but the difference may be only a few bucks when all is said and done. I don't really have a preference which approach you use. If you are a total math nerd and are obsessed over interest rates, then go with that option. If you are tired of having several little debts buzzing around your head like mosquitoes and want some quick wins, go by balance. Either way, you'll be working toward the goal of becoming debt-free.

Once you've paid off the credit cards, commit to never carrying a balance again. If you want to use a credit card for convenience, perks, or air miles, that's fine, but pay it off every month. You have more important things to do with your money than to donate it to the bank in the form of interest payments. And yes, paying as you go means you can't simply buy whatever you want whenever you want it, but that's OK. You're working toward a day when you can literally buy *anything you want*, including resort hotels in the Bahamas! Enjoy your life, but keep the end in sight.

One strategy I have used is carrying cash and not using a credit card except for gas, hotels, or car rentals. It amazing how much less you spend when you have to count real cash and hand it to a vendor instead of mindlessly swiping a piece of plastic. This single change in behavior can reduce your spending as much as 30 percent and put you on the fast track to savings and debt reduction. If you use a card online, I also suggest taking a good look at your monthly statement. Look for reoccurring charges for subscriptions, memberships, and services you don't use. Gym memberships, magazines, Spotify, Netflix, Hulu, YouTube TV, cable service ... all these monthly payments are killing the average family. Cut out the ones you don't need. Every dollar you *don't* spend is like getting a $1.40 raise because the money you have and keep has already been taxed. Most employees can give themselves a huge pay raise just by clearing out the subscription clutter from their credit card bill.

Now what about car debt? I think car loans are fine for a season, but they should never be an accepted part of your life from now to eternity. If you need to borrow money to buy a car, keep the loan to three years or less. Don't even think about these crazy five-, six-, or even seven-year car loans that have become the norm over the past twenty years. If you need seven years to pay off your car, you're buying cars you can't afford. If you really want to think out of the box, why don't you pay your car off in three years and then keep saving that same car payment in a separate car fund every month for another three years?

At that point, you've got a six-year-old car that might need to be replaced, but you've also got enough money to buy your next one with cash. Or if you're buying cars every six years or so, you could alternate between car payments and extra investing by paying car payments for three years, then sending that same amount to your investing accounts for the next three years, then buying a car and starting the process over. This helps you maintain a car-sized allocation in your monthly spending every year while giving you the benefit of investing tens of thousands more dollars over your working lifetime!

Speaking as a car enthusiast, I used to be more excited about the *idea* of buying fancy cars than I was with the *reality*. In fact, one of the saddest days of my life was the day I drove my brand-new Mercedes home from the dealership. This was a planned purchase as a reward for hitting an income goal. Driving it home, though, I felt sad. I wondered, *Is this all there is to a Mercedes?* I was still in college at the time, but I was driving the same car doctors and lawyers were driving. And it felt . . . hollow. I realized I was equating "stuff" and external recognition with financial security. But they're not the same. My financial security was in my account, and I wasted much of it on a high-end depreciating asset. I didn't enjoy the journey but pinned all my hope on the destination, and I came away disappointed. Five miles from the dealership, I thought, *It's been five minutes, and this thing is already worth a lot less than I owe on it.* From that point on, I decided to buy nice cars only if I could pay cash for them and still have a reserve. I also check myself to see what emotional bucket I may be trying to satisfy or if it's a fun idea that doesn't set me back. The funny thing is, when I have enough cash on hand to pay for a really nice car, I'd usually rather invest it than drive it.

If I haven't stepped on your toes yet with credit cards and cars, how about this one: student loans. Too many people think student loans are as inevitable and interminable as car payments. They're wrong on both counts. The average US household with student loan debt owes $57,520.[9] If you're sitting there owing tens of thousands in student loan debt, and if you're planning on making the piddly minimum payments for the rest of your life, you're choosing to limit both your wealth building and your peace of mind. Cut your budget to the bone, skip the luxuries, and double, triple, or quadruple your loan payments. You paid a lot for that education; now it's time to put it work. Use it to pull yourself out of the hole you're in, lift your sights, think big, and get out of debt.

Step 4: Invest in Roth IRAs and Growth Mutual Funds

So, what are you investing in? The first thing, as we've seen, is to take advantage of the company match on a 401(k)—especially if it's a Roth 401(k)—if you have that option available. Once you max out the match, stop putting money into the 401(k) and open a Roth IRA.

A Roth IRA is a retirement account that grows absolutely tax-free, meaning you'll pay zero in taxes at retirement when you start pulling money out of the account. There's almost nothing else like this; it's basically a gift from the federal government, and it's a gift that could ultimately be worth hundreds of thousands of dollars or more. The trade-off is that you will invest *after-tax dollars*, meaning you bring the money home first, and then you'll deposit the funds into your

Roth account. That means you'll effectively be investing less than you would in a pre-tax vehicle like a 401(k) because to bring $100 home you really need to earn about $130 to cover taxes. However, the tax-free growth you'll gain on that $100 still makes it the better deal.

There are three main restrictions to know about the Roth IRA. First, there's a limit to how much you can put into a Roth each year. The fact that you're allowed to put a lot more into a 401(k) than a Roth shows you that the Roth is a much better deal for you and not nearly as good a deal for the government. As of 2021, a working adult can contribute up to $6,000 per year ($7,000 if age fifty or older) into a Roth. Married couples can each have a Roth, even if one spouse doesn't have an earned income, and each partner can contribute up to the max. This means a married couple can save $12,000 per year (or $14,000 if age fifty or older) and enjoy tax-free growth all the way to retirement.

Second, because this is a retirement account, you are not able to withdraw funds without substantial taxes and penalties until age fifty-nine and a half. There are a handful of exceptions to this rule, such as pulling money out for a down payment as a first-time home-buyer or expenses resulting from birth or adoption, but I would not even consider this possibility. Your retirement funds are there to *fund your retirement*. The Roth isn't a piggy bank, so don't crack it open early.

Third, there's a chance you don't qualify for a Roth IRA if you have a high income. As of 2021, married couples filing jointly with a household income under $198,000 can contribute the maximum $6,000 per spouse. If the household income is $198,000–$208,000, married couples filing jointly can contribute a reduced amount. If the household income is above $208,000, married couples filing jointly are ineligible for the Roth IRA altogether. Single taxpayers have similar rules with different limits: full contribution up to $125,000 income, reduced contribution if making $125,000–$140,000 in income, and ineligible over $140,000 income. Of course, these rules change over time, so make sure to speak with a financial professional. Any qualified financial advisor can walk you through this and set you up with a Roth IRA.

One more point on the Roth IRA, and something most people overlook, is that you have some ability to choose the assets inside the Roth IRA. This little detail became big news as I'm writing this, when the media discovered that entrepreneur and investor Peter Thiel had a Roth IRA balance of $5 *billion*! This is unheard of. Thiel, the cofounder of PayPal, used his Roth IRA to buy 1.7 million shares of PayPal for $0.001 per share, or $1,700 total (the Roth IRA had a $2,000 annual contribution limit at that time). His balance in just the Roth IRA hit $5 billion in 2021, when Thiel was fifty-three years old.[10] As long as he doesn't touch it for another seven years, he'll be able to withdraw those funds after age fifty-nine and a half and pay absolutely no taxes on all those billions of dollars of growth. Sure, this is an incredible example, but it's a good reminder of your ability to choose your favorite assets inside the Roth. It's definitely something to discuss with your advisor as you make your contributions.

If you take the 401(k) match and max out your Roth IRA and *still* have money left to invest, talk to your financial advisor about growth mutual funds. These give you a good way to invest in the stock market without taking on all the risks associated with single stocks. There are still no guarantees, of course, but mutual funds enable you to hedge your bets by investing in several companies at once. We'll talk about mutual funds and other market-based securities in chapter 11. But first, let's not miss my favorite type of investing for wealth building.

Step 5: Invest in Real Estate

I love real estate, and there's a good reason for that: real estate has created more billionaires and millionaires in this country than any other investment vehicle. And much of that wealth has been created with the investor using only a little of his or her own money. You think your employer's 401(k) match is great? Just wait until you buy an investment property using mostly someone else's money! Unlike other investments, real estate has distinct tax advantages that allow you to borrow 60, 70, or even 95 percent of the purchase price of a property and then write off the costs of the loan as an expense on your taxes. That's right: use other people's money and write off what you pay to use their money.

Real estate can be such a huge factor to your long-term wealth building that I'll devote an entire chapter to it. For now, it's enough to say that real estate is awesome, it's easier than you think, and it can make you rich with just a little effort—if you know how to play the game.

Step 6: Save for College Using 529 Plans

Emergencies, retirement, and wealth building aren't the only things you need to be saving for. If you have young children, you should already be planning how to pay for their college expenses. The cost of college has become absolutely ridiculous over the past thirty years. For the 2020–2021 school year, the average "sticker price" for one year at a four-year state school for in-state residents was $26,820, which included tuition, fees, room, and board. Throw in books and supplies, and the figure rises to over $31,000—*per year*.[11] That puts the price of a four-year degree at around $125,000. If you go to an out-of-state school or, heaven forbid, a private university, you'll see that cost skyrocket even more. Some private colleges are over $75,000 a year, bringing your four-year total to $300,000 or more.

Education has become a seemingly insurmountable burden for the typical American family. I have five boys. Financial aid and scholarships notwithstanding, it's entirely possible that all their college degrees and potential advanced degrees combined will hit or exceed $1 million!

Colleges present all kinds of financial aid packages as options, but most of that "help" will be in the form of student loans. We as a nation owe $1.57 *trillion* in outstanding student loan debt, and 14 percent of *all adults* in this country are currently paying off student loans. Like I said above, today's graduates are jumping into the career waters with an anchor tied around their legs. I don't think anyone wants their adult children to begin life in massive debt.

There's not much we can do about the cost of college, but we can at least prepare for it. The best way to do that, in my opinion, is the 529 plan. The 529 works much like a Roth IRA except it is designed exclusively for education expenses. Parents or grandparents are allowed to open a 529 for each child from birth, and I encourage you to do so. I opened one for each of my boys as soon as they were born. You invest after-tax dollars, but the investment grows tax-free. As long as you use the funds for approved educational expenses, you won't pay a cent in taxes when you pull the money out.

Each state runs its own 529 plan, and therefore the rules governing maximum contributions vary from state to state. However, it's important to note that you don't *have* to open a 529 governed by the state you live in. Just because I live in South Carolina doesn't mean I have to open a South Carolina 529. I can shop around and select the plan that best fits my needs. While each state has different maximum contribution limits, the beauty of the 529 (besides growing tax-free) is that the maximum lifetime contributions are high enough to cover pretty much any educational need. Georgia and Mississippi have the lowest limits at $235,000, and California has the highest at $529,000. Your financial advisor can help you identify the plan that works best for you and your student's needs.

I recommend parents open a 529 as early as possible and commit to making regular contributions every month. It can be hard to see college as a priority when your child is still in diapers, but investing early gives you the power of compound interest. Besides, unlike your retirement savings, you have only about eighteen years to save up for your child's college. That gives compound interest less time to work its magic, which makes your contributions even more important.

In addition to your monthly contributions, you can invite others to make one-off deposits into your child's 529 plan. For example, you might ask the grandparents to make a 529 contribution for birthdays and Christmases instead of buying more plastic junk that will end up stuffed in a closet (or broken in the trash) after a month. All those $50 or $100 gifts from birth to age eighteen can make a huge difference alongside Mom and Dad's monthly contributions.

INCOME MANAGEMENT FOR ENTREPRENEURS

If you're self-employed or a business owner, you almost certainly do not have a regular, set, steady paycheck hitting your bank account every two weeks like most people. That gives you what's called an *irregular income*, meaning you get paid different amounts at different times. You might get a $40,000 check from a client one week and then nothing else for a few months. Depending on your personality, you could find this prospect either terrifying or thrilling. In either case, the basic action plan for entrepreneurial income is:

1. Prepare for emergencies with cash reserves and insurance.
2. Pay off your credit cards.
3. Invest in your business.
4. Invest in a Simplified Employee Pension (SEP) plan.
5. Invest into Roth IRAs.
6. Invest in real estate.
7. Save for your children's college with 529 plans.

Managing this type of income isn't that dissimilar from what we previously discussed, but there are a few important differences you need to be aware of. Let's take a look.

Step 1: Prepare for Emergencies with Cash Reserves and Insurance

Your need for a basic savings account to cover emergencies is the same as what we discussed. With no steady income, though, you'll need to stay on the higher end of savings. I recommend aiming at six months' worth of expenses set aside. This should help you weather any gaps in income along with any unexpected expenses.

Now, six months of savings should cover your *personal* needs, but what about your business? Depending on what type of work you do, you might also need to save three to six months' worth of expenses for the business on top of your personal savings. This is called *retained earnings*. This is to help your business survive during dry spells and cover any business-related emergency expenses. For example, if you and a buddy run a lawn care company, you depend on your equipment to do your work. If your mower breaks down, you can't cut any yards. Fixing or replacing that machine suddenly becomes your A-1 priority, and you need the cash on hand to get it back in service or replace it immediately. Every day it's out of commission costs you money, so having sufficient retained earnings—savings—will mean the difference between having a bad *day* and a bad *outcome*.

When heavy equipment is involved, you definitely need to have more in savings or a standby line of credit with a bank that you draw on only in emergencies as you build your reserve. But plan for this well in advance. Lines of credit are easy to get when you *don't* need money and hard to get when you *do*. Mark Twain said, "A banker is a fellow who lends you his umbrella when the sun is shining, but wants it back the minute it begins to rain." Good words to remember.

On the other end of the spectrum might be a freelance creative professional. A writer, for example, may depend only on his laptop to get his work done. Assuming he has sufficient personal savings, this type of entrepreneur could probably get away with only a month or two of expenses held in savings. As long as he has enough in the bank to replace a busted computer in an emergency, his work can carry on largely uninterrupted. Every entrepreneur's needs are a little different, so take a close look at exactly what it would take to keep your business afloat in an emergency and make sure you put that much in the bank.

Additionally, as a business owner, you need to be extremely careful about putting the right types of insurance in place. This is just as important as having money in the bank. At a minimum, I'd expect you to need keyman insurance, disability, and general liability coverages. Get with a good insurance professional to discuss your needs in detail.

Step 2: Pay Off All Debt except Cars and Mortgages

Too often, people with irregular incomes use credit cards to make up for their lack of planning. *No income? No problem! We'll just charge our groceries, gas, and entertainment this month!* Bad, bad idea. Your savings are designed to catch your income lulls and emergencies; do not depend on debt for your basic living expenses!

Lines of credit can be very helpful in growing a business, but they can also easily get out of hand when used incorrectly. I seem to meet only two types of people: those who have tons of available credit they never use and those who have tons of credit completely maxed out. Can you guess which ones are wealthier?

Refer to what I said about debt, credit cards, car loans, and student loans. This applies to the entrepreneur just as much as it does to the employee.

Step 3: Invest in Your Business

I had lunch recently with a dear friend who owns a small business with three work trucks (all on loans) and three independent contractors who work for him. My friend runs absolutely everything about the business. He answers the phone. He does all the marketing. He does the accounting. He schedules the regular service on the trucks. He does all the follow-up with customers. He maintains the website. He even orders the office supplies and makes sure there's paper in the copier. This guy does *everything* . . . and it's killing him. As we talked, he complained that the business wasn't growing, and I replied, "Yeah, no kidding. Do you want to know why it's not growing? It's because the owner is spending all day, every day running in circles taking care of the little things, and no one is driving the big things. If you want to grow, you've got to invest in the business and hire an office manager to take all that off your plate!"

That brings me to Step 3. This step may require a paradigm shift for you, but I believe one of the most significant, most valuable investments any entrepreneur can make is an investment in the business itself. Say you own a small print shop that you've been running as a one-man show for the past few years with gross revenues of $250,000. If you had $50,000 to invest, you *could* put it in a marketable security like a mutual fund or retirement account. It might earn a 10 or 12 percent rate of return over time, which is fine. Or you could invest that $50,000 into the business by hiring someone to run the shop while you focus on sales and growing the business. If that employee freed you up to work *on* the business instead of just *in* the business, you could double or triple your revenues in a year.

In this example, what's the rate of return for the $50,000 you invested into the business? It's a lot more than 12 percent! If you doubled your sales and took your business from $250,000 to $500,000 in revenue simply by hiring someone to handle the day-to-day work while you focus on bigger things, you'd effectively be getting a 500 percent rate of return on your $50,000 investment! Trust me, you're not going to beat that in the stock market.

What else might investing in your business look like? If you owned the lawn care company I discussed, it might mean buying a more efficient mower that enabled you to cut more yards in a day. If you were a video editor, it might mean upgrading your computer so your projects could render twice as fast. If you're in sales, it might mean updating your wardrobe and replacing your worn-out car to present a more professional appearance for potential clients. If you lead a small team, it might mean attending a leadership workshop or networking event. It might even mean something as simple as buying a $12 book on a new sales technique or a $20 pack of thank-you cards for your customers. These are things we often take for granted and hesitate spending money on, but each of these things adds value to your business. Even taking your biggest customers out to eat, golfing, bowling, river rafting, motorcycle riding, go-cart racing, or hosting them at your home for dinner can be tremendous investments. You'd be surprised how a simple gesture can totally change you relationship and your business.

One warning though: it's easy to use "investing in the business" as an excuse to buy toys you don't really need. If it doesn't create new revenue, it's an *expense*, not an investment. Every dollar you spend on the business should come back to you two-, ten-, or twentyfold. If it doesn't, you're just wasting money.

Step 4: Invest in a Simplified Employee Pension (SEP) Plan

One downside of running your own business is missing out on the potential for an employer match on 401(k) contributions. Again, there's nothing like free money to motivate you to save! However, entrepreneurs aren't completely left out in the cold when it comes to retirement plans. In fact, business owners—even solopreneurs— may have an even better option than their timeclock-punching friends.

The Simplified Employee Pension (SEP) plan is a retirement vehicle specifically designed for business owners—even if you are the business's only employee. It works much like a traditional 401(k) and has a similar tax treatment, wherein you invest pre-tax dollars into a SEP-IRA and pay the taxes on the back end when you withdraw funds at retirement. However, because you're both the employer *and* the employee, you get to be as generous as you want with yourself with the company match—up to a point.

As an employee of your own company, you can contribute what- ever you want into the SEP. Then, as the employer, you can offer a company match on employee contributions. However, whereas a typical company may offer a 3 or 4 percent match, the SEP enables you to give yourself a 1:1 match up to 25 percent of your income! No 401(k) plan can come close to this.

There are two caveats to be aware of. First, the SEP employer matching contributions max out at 25 percent of the employee's income or $58,000 (whichever is less) as of 2021. Second, and this is huge if you employ anyone else, every full-time employee must have access to the SEP plan and every participant has to receive the same match. So if you set up a SEP for your business and have one or more employees who participate, they'll get whatever match you give yourself. That is, you can't give yourself a 25 percent match and give your employees a 4 percent match. SEPs are designed for small operations, and you're all in it together.

SEPs are not perfect, but they are fantastic investing options for business owners and solopreneurs. I recommend talking to your financial advisor about this before you do any other open-market investing.

Steps 5, 6, and 7: Roth, Real Estate, and College Savings

The remaining steps are the same for the entrepreneur as they are for the employee:

1. Invest in Roth IRAs.
2. Invest in real estate.
3. Save for your children's college with 529 plans.

Follow the recommendations I've outlined and/or talk to your financial pro about these items, and you'll be covered.

MAKE YOURSELF INDISPENSABLE

We covered a lot of ground in this chapter, and I hope I gave you a solid list of action items for growing and managing your income no matter what position or industry you're in. Building wealth can be as easy or as complicated as you want it to be. Nothing I discussed here is too complicated on the surface, but each of these topics could uncover a thousand different rabbit trails. For this reason, I strongly encourage you to work with a trusted financial advisor who can walk alongside you for the long haul, point out new opportunities, and warn you about any upcoming pitfalls. This kind of one-on-one guidance is so important, especially if you're just starting out.

As I close this chapter, I want to give you one final piece of advice about growing your income, and it applies whether you're an employee or an entrepreneur: *make yourself indispensable.* The best way to ensure a healthy, growing income is to become absolutely essential to your company and customers.

If you're an employee, that means making yourself indispensable to your boss by making him or her look good. That may sound crass, but it's true. The best form of job security is being the one person the boss can't afford to lose. If you can make your employer's job easier, he or she is more likely to go to bat for you when it comes to pay raises and/or potential layoffs. So, don't be the employee who shows up a few minutes late every day, does the bare minimum, keeps his head down, and watches the clock until 5:00 p.m. Instead, be the one who is there to greet the boss every morning when he or she arrives, finishes every task with excellence on time or early, knows all the power players in the company, and knows how to get stuff done. Most people are coasting through the day, so it doesn't take much to outshine everyone else. Just a little bit of effort will go a long way.

Invest in yourself. Read books. Listen to audiobooks and podcasts while you're in your car, working out, or even on the job if possible. Select titles on customer service, management, sales, business development, and leadership, even if you don't see the direct relevance to your job. The truth is, *everyone* is in customer service, management, sales, and leadership regardless of what their job title is. We all need to get better at working with other people. We could all learn a thing or two about becoming more efficient. We're all selling *something*— even if it's just selling ourselves by proving how valuable we are to the company's bottom line. Whatever you do, wherever you are, be the one person who is irreplaceable and watch your income soar!

If you're an entrepreneur, your job is to become indispensable to your customers. Provide a service no one else can match in terms of quality and performance. Be proactive about meeting their needs. Don't just do what they hired you to do; do it better than anyone else. Force them with your excellence to keep you top-of-mind whenever they need someone in your field. Win them over every chance you get, never forgetting that you are competing for their business against a world full of other hard-charging entrepreneurs who are just waiting for you to screw something up. Don't get lazy, always send thank-you notes and birthday cards, entertain your clients, and just be thoughtful and intentional in everything you do. You can easily take control of your market because most of your competitors are happy to do the bare minimum. But not you!

As I write this in the spring of 2021, I'm looking back on a crazy year marked by unprecedented global lockdowns and a pandemic-wrecked economy. The professional landscape has never faced what we've been through over the past twelve months. Yet it's shocking to me how many people I know who didn't just *survive* during this time, they *thrived*. They made themselves indispensable to their companies and customers at a time when others were shrinking back and, in return, many of them had the best year of their lives. That's what I want for you, and you can do it by following the handful of action steps I've outlined here.

CHAPTER 9

The Benefits of Real Estate

I mentioned earlier that the whole concept of "who's eating your pie?" began when I was trying to teach my son about taxes. It was the best illustration I could come up with to explain what it's like when the government swoops in and gobbles up 30 or 40 percent of your hard-earned income. I believe without a doubt that taxes—along with various fees placed on investments—are the two biggest threats to your long-term wealth creation. So, as we're looking for strategies to not only *build* but *protect* our financial pie, I'm always going to favor wealth-building tools that are tax- and fee-efficient.

We've seen the benefits of tax-*free* options like Roth IRAs and 529 college savings plans, which tax the seed instead of the harvest. We've also looked at tax-*favored* options like the 401(k), which tax the harvest instead of the seed. These are both good options, but what if there was a way to avoid or minimize income taxes and fees altogether?

Enter real estate.

Real estate is an oasis in the tax-crazed world of investing. It is hands-down the best way to build wealth that you actually get to *keep* instead of splitting with the government. The federal tax code has more incentives and benefits for real estate investors than any other form of investing. There's no doubt that's why more millionaires are made through real estate than anything else, a fact that has stood the test of time. More than a century ago, Andrew Carnegie, one of the wealthiest men in history, declared,

> Ninety percent of all millionaires become so through owning real estate. More money has been made in real estate than in all industrial investments combined. The wise young man or wage earner of today invests his money in real estate.

If it was good enough for Carnegie, it's good enough for me.

Real estate has been very good to me over the years—both for myself and for others. I couldn't even tell you how many properties my clients or I have owned off the top of my head. I've been buying or developing with partners in real estate for thirty years, with some properties worth over $100 million. I own many by myself, and I own many more in partnership with others. I've covered the spectrum of real estate options, including residential, multifamily, industrial, storage, restaurants, retail, hotels, office space, and parking space. Name a type of building sitting on a patch of dirt in America, and I likely have some experience in that asset class, some good and some bad. Experience is just that, and everything doesn't work during every economic cycle. The most important takeaway is to keep trying and keep moving ahead over time. Real estate rewards persistence.

Real estate gives you more types of investment opportunities, more flexibility in ownership, more tax benefits, more ways of financing, more access to other people's money (OPM), and more profit potential than any other type of investing—period. If you're serious about building wealth and protecting your pie from taxes, it's time to get familiar with real estate.

Of course, there are whole books, courses, and workshops on how to invest in real estate, so there's no way I can tell you *everything* you need to know in one or two chapters. Instead, my goal in this and the following chapter is to run through the basics. I just want to whet your appetite by covering the benefits, explaining a few different ways to make money, and showing you what's possible through real estate investing. Plus, I'll give you some simple steps for starting your own real estate investing journey. It may seem scary and complicated, but trust me . . . *anyone* can do this. And, in my opinion, most should.

THE UNIQUE BENEFITS OF REAL ESTATE

Real estate is perhaps the single most flexible investment category. You can be as involved as you want to be. If you have time and interest, you can do all the work yourself, from finding the property to managing needed renovations to renting it out to managing the property yourself. Or if you just want the benefits of real estate investing without any of the work, you could be more of a silent partner who funds deals for another investor who has the time and interest to get in the weeds. If you're concerned about liquidity—being able to cash out quickly—you could skip owning properties yourself and instead invest in companies that invest in real estate through a marketable security or mutual fund that offers daily liquidity. There's a wide spectrum full of opportunities for everyone.

Regardless of what role you choose to play in your real estate investing, there are many benefits that make this a great tool for growing your financial pie. Let's run through some of the big ones.

A Familiar, Physical Asset

Many people distrust market-based investments because it all seems so intangible and mysterious. The typical person has no idea why a stock might be worth $100 one day and $85 or $115 the next. And we've all seen the nightmare headlines about how people's entire retirement savings were severely impacted overnight for no clear reason, or at least no reason you'd expect to impact that company for any length of time. Sudden market drops might be tied to political events, elections, civil unrest, or just how the wind is blowing one day. It can be impossible to see any rhyme or reason to it at all. Sometimes the entire stock market can look like a house of cards— or, even worse, like an *invisible* house of cards.

Real estate, however, is more cut-and-dried. People *get* the act of buying a property—usually a single-family home—and making payments on it over time until they own it outright. They're familiar with the concept of appreciation. They know what it's like to rent a house or an apartment from someone else. They understand that retail stores and corporations lease their office space. In this, real estate isn't invisible like a stock certificate; it's a familiar, physical asset. They can *see* the house they purchased. They can walk through the rooms, put their hands on the walls, and say, "I own this." This alone makes real estate an attractive option for many people who find it hard to trust an investment strategy they can't see or touch.

I can hop in my car and drive by many different properties within thirty minutes of my house. I can see the condition of the roof. I can see if the tenants are taking care of the yard. If there were bad storms the night before, I can see if my properties were damaged and in need of repair. You just can't do that with market-based securities. Plus, I know there are things I can do to raise the value of any physical asset I hold. A coat of paint, new carpet, and some landscaping don't just make the house look better; they also make it worth more.

Imagine using $10,000 from a home equity line of credit to turn your back patio into a sunroom. The HELOC may cost you 4 percent in interest, or $400 a year. However, that $10,000 sunroom adds $15,000 to the overall value of your home. That's an immediate 50 percent return on your money. You're paying the bank 4 percent but making 50 percent! Real estate is the only investing option that consistently gives you that kind of flexibility and potential return. Even better, if you make this upgrade to a rental home, the tenant is actually paying for the sunroom through their rent payments! In this example, you literally *created* $15,000 in value out of nothing!

You ever try to add a sunroom to a mutual fund? It doesn't work as well.

Someone Else Pays Off Your Mortgage

You may have scratched your head just now when I said the tenant paid for the sunroom in the preceding example. Here's what I meant: one of the most incredible benefits of real estate is that you can purchase a rental property with a little money down and the rest on a mortgage, and then you can pay off that mortgage with *someone else's money.* Say you own a rental home with a $150,000 mortgage. Your mortgage payment is $850 a month, but your renter is paying you $1,200 in rent. If you have the rent payments automatically deposited and the mortgage payments automatically deducted from your bank account, your renter is literally paying your mortgage payments every month without you having to do anything!

Plus, if you own that house for the full fifteen or thirty years it takes to naturally pay off the mortgage, two other things are going to happen while your renter pays off your loan. First, your rental income will likely go up 2 or 3 percent every year with inflation. If you start by collecting $1,400 in rent, you'll be collecting much more than that several years later. Second, while your rental income is going up, your mortgage payment (with a fixed-rate mortgage) will stay the same. Even if your rent shoots up to $2,000 a month over time, you'll still owe the same $850 to the bank. This leaves you with even more cash flow every month to save, live on, use to pay off the mortgage faster, or use to invest in more properties. Other people are literally paying off your investment properties and giving you tremendous monthly cash flow—all while they enjoy a safe, nice place to live that you provided.

Another thing about using renters' money to pay off your mortgage is that you can almost always find someone to rent your house. When the housing market is hot, meaning people are buying houses like crazy, you'd expect the rental market to dip, but that has never happened to me. In fact, my rentals do better in a hot market than they do in a slow one. On the flip side, you have periods when the housing market gets shaky and we're experiencing high foreclosure rates because homebuyers made some stupid financing decisions. The rental market is great then, too, because those people who are losing their homes need to find a new place to live. So whether the market is hot or cold, I have no problem finding quality renters who need a good home and who are grateful for the chance to pay rent!

Tax Incentives

Investing in real estate is also unique compared to other investments in the tax advantages offered by the federal government. These tax breaks are offered to promote homeownership, provide affordable housing for people at all income levels, bring stability to communities, encourage investors to take risks with capital, and create jobs in construction and other industries. While market-based securities like stocks are taxed into oblivion, the tax laws heavily favor real estate investors. To ignore that fantastic benefit is detrimental to your financial health.

These benefits begin with what's traditionally your first real estate purchase: the home you live in. There are first-time homebuyer programs that enable you to purchase a home with as little as 3 percent down under specific government programs. That means you can buy a $150,000 house with only $4,500 out-of-pocket in some communities (assuming you have good credit). Of course, putting that little down on a home comes with other risks, which we'll discuss later, but this is just one example of how the government incentivizes homeownership.

Once you make the jump into real estate investing for wealth building, you'll discover all manner of perfectly legal and acceptable ways to shield your income from taxes. I know real estate millionaires who pay practically nothing in income taxes. Nothing! How is that possible? It's because of government-offered incentives such as the

1031 exchange and depreciation, both of which we'll discuss. And when I say real estate investors can avoid paying income taxes, be sure to notice the word *income*. I am absolutely not saying we can avoid paying *all* taxes. As a real estate investor, I can use all the legal means of avoiding income taxes, but I'm still paying property taxes on every property every year. That's why it drives me crazy when people on TV complain about the "evil rich people" who don't pay any taxes. What about the millions these people pay in property taxes, payroll taxes, corporate taxes, wealth taxes, sales taxes, and all the other ways the government sticks their fingers in other people's financial pies? Real estate investors may not pay much in taxes on their real estate income, but they are taxed into oblivion everywhere else. Like it or not, that's how the tax code is set up.

There's a lot of talk these days about whether it's moral to use these methods of tax avoidance, but I don't think morality has anything to do with it. The bottom line is that the government *freely offers* these incentives to real estate investors. Congress wrote the tax code and breaking those rules, of course, is wrong. However, there is *nothing* wrong with using every legal method of avoiding or minimizing taxes. After all, tax receipts only go up as real estate developers transform properties to meet current demand trends and thus stimulate tax revenue. That's why developers get tax breaks: at the end of the day, they are helping create jobs, tax revenues, and opportunities for many.

These benefits are there for one reason: to encourage more people to invest in their communities by purchasing, building, and improving the homes and commercial buildings in the area. And real estate does much more than provide places to live and work; real estate as an industry creates more jobs than almost anything else. It's one of the leading economic drivers in the country, creating jobs in construction, manufacturing, production, electronics, pest control, heating and air, plumbing, landscaping, and dozens of other industries. The more properties I own, the more jobs I help support throughout the US economy. And the more I save on taxes, the more money I have to buy more properties, keeping the cycle going and growing. Not taking advantage of the government's tax incentives isn't just bad personal financial management; it's bad for the economy as a whole. They're there for a reason. Use them.

I should also say here that I am not a tax expert; I've just owned enough real estate that I've gotten pretty familiar with the ins and outs of the game. Of course, once you're ready to start investing in real estate yourself, you'll want to have several conversations with a quality CPA or tax pro who specializes in working with real estate investors.

Avoid All Taxes Through a 1031 Exchange

One of the best tax advantages available to real estate investors is the 1031 exchange. This is a benefit that literally makes taxes optional when you make a profit selling an investment property. Here's how it works: Say you purchased a property for $200,000 five years ago. You've paid the loan down $20,000 since then using your rental income, and the home's value has increased $40,000. Now, you want to sell it. You've technically made $60,000 ($20,000 in loan repayment and $40,000 in appreciation), so you'd normally expect to pay taxes on that appreciation, right? Not so with a 1031 exchange!

Using this option, you can sell that home and use *all* the proceeds to buy a different property within a specified time frame without paying a cent in taxes. You can then let that new house build value while the renter pays your loan down again, and then you can do *another* 1031 exchange. And then another. You can repeat this cycle as many times as you want, upgrading from one home to the next and using all those saved tax dollars to continue building your net worth. You can literally create a multimillion-dollar net worth and never pay taxes. Then, when you die, you can leave those properties to your heirs, and they can keep the ball rolling by getting a stepped-up basis based on the date of your death, meaning their gains are based on the value of the property at the time they take ownership upon your death, not at the time you originally purchased the property.

Compare this to buying and selling stocks. Every time you sell a marketable security at a profit, you pay capital gains taxes. Every single time. There's no way to avoid it. But with a 1031 exchange, you *never* have to pay taxes on your real estate gains. It's a night-and-day difference. There's nothing else like it in the world of investing. Again, I'm not a CPA or tax expert, so you'll want to consult a professional tax advisor if/when you're ready to take advantage of a 1031 exchange.

Appreciation and Depreciation

A friend was riding through town with his grandfather recently, discussing how much the area had grown over the past several years. Once considered "the outskirts of town," it was now the go-to destination for trendy shops, restaurants, hotels, and a handful of large chain retail stores. When they passed a big, new shopping mall, my friend's grandfather pointed and said, "You know, this was all empty farmland when I was your age. I actually had the chance to buy all this property for $5,000 back then, but I didn't want to risk losing my money. Who could have guessed it would grow into *this*?"

I could have.

I'm not bragging, but I could have predicted the area's development over the decades. I know this because everything breaks down to supply and demand. When an area is experiencing population growth, it's inevitable that real estate will increase in value. Real estate is like a net present value machine that calculates the highest and best use for the property, and that becomes the new market value. For example, if farming is the highest value, then things like grass, quality soil, access to water, and labor are drivers. However, once a shopping center or a subdivision goes in nearby, it's always back to supply and demand and what would serve the area best now. Pads for a Starbucks to build on are worth about one hundred times what farmland is per acre. So, buy property where the change is coming and enjoy this for yourself.

That's what real estate does: It goes up in value over time. Property is simply worth more today than it was twenty, thirty, or a hundred years ago. It *appreciates*—even if it's just a piece of dirt. Why? Because they aren't making any more land! All we've got now is all there will ever be. As communities grow, people will need places to live, work, and play. Think how much different and bigger the world seems to be today compared to your grandparents' generation. Now think what the world will look like for *your* grandchildren. Do you think that future generation will need *less* land, homes, commercial property, parking spots, and storage facilities? Heck, no! The march of progress pushes us forward, which in turn pushes the value of real estate right along with it.

The median US home value in 1970 was about $17,000. In 2020, it was $320,000.[12] To be honest, that figure shocked me. I had to triple-check it to make sure I was looking at the right number. Even adjusted for inflation, the value of the median home has more than doubled in the past fifty years. And that's not just the sticks and bricks that make up the home itself; a big part of the value is the land that house is sitting on. There's no telling what could have happened if my friend's grandfather had pulled together the $5,000 he needed to buy that piece of land all those years ago. That could have been the key that unlocked generational wealth for every member of his family for the next century or more.

If you're reading this and you're in your twenties or thirties, just imagine what your retirement could look like if you paid today's prices for a dozen rental properties. You'd be sitting on a multi-million-dollar net worth with properties other people (your renters) paid off as you sat back and watched it happen. Then you could pass those properties to your heirs and leave this world knowing you left them an inheritance that will keep growing as long as they hang on to them. That is an amazing legacy.

Unbelievably, while you watch your property values go up over time, you can write them off as losses on your taxes as you claim *depreciation*. For practical purposes, depreciation means *useful life* in the tax code. Physical buildings, like a home, experience wear and tear over time. The roof ages, the foundation shifts, the HVAC wears out, the drywall rots. These things cause the book value of your property to decrease each year—even though the actual value of your home is likely increasing. That gives you a hedge against taxes and, in some cases, can completely shelter your real estate income.

For example, let's say you own a rental property that collects $1,000 in rent. After your mortgage and other expenses, you're left with $200 profit each month. Normally, you'd owe taxes on that profit. However, if you follow the letter of the tax code and set a depreciation schedule for the property, you can deduct the depreciation, creating a paper loss that offsets the taxes you'd otherwise owe. From a wealth-building perspective, your value is increasing, and from a tax perspective, your value is decreasing. As an investor, you get the benefit of both!

If you sell the house and pocket the proceeds instead of using a 1031 exchange to roll those funds into another property, you'll owe a portion of those depreciated tax savings back to the government. However, by pushing this tax hit off as long as possible, you get to keep more of your money and use those tax savings to build an even bigger portfolio. So, use a 1031 if available. As I write this, there is talk about removing a tax-free exchange from the tax law. Again, though, consult a tax pro for the nuts and bolts of how to claim depreciation correctly.

Growing Your Portfolio

Buying your first rental property can be scary (we'll talk about *how* to buy), but that first purchase will get the ball rolling. Let's say you scrape together $20,000 to put down on your first house. Then, as we saw, you sell it five years later after paying the mortgage down $20,000 and the house has appreciated $20,000. When you sell, you get your original $20,000 back plus the equity you gained through the mortgage repayment *plus* the equity you gained through appreciation. So after five years, your original $20,000 has grown to $60,000. At that point, you can do exactly what you did the first time, only now you have enough money to put $20,000 down on three different houses! This gives you three properties that are appreciating and three renters who are paying down your three mortgages. You can let this go another few years and repeat the cycle, using your profits from appreciation and mortgage pay down to buy even more houses. The first time, you went from one house to three. Now, using the same numbers in our example, you can go from three to nine! You can repeat the cycle as many times as you want, growing a multimillion-dollar net worth—and it all started with that original $20,000 investment on your first property.

And what happens along the way? You learn all about real estate. You build relationships with banks, lenders, and real estate investors who are impressed by your hard work and track record. You figure out how involved you want to be in the process and develop systems to maximize your time. You develop a reputation as someone who's improving their community and providing beautiful homes for people. And, as you grow your reputation, you grow new opportunities to invest in new ways and on a larger scale. For example, as people watch your success over time, they may want to come alongside you and partner with you on some deals. Someone who has money to invest but no time to spend on the deal could offer to fund a property if you'll manage all the details. This is called a joint venture, and I and many others do them all the time. You could have someone who puts in the $20,000 needed to buy a home, but you buy it together in a 50/50 deal. Then, you find the property, oversee any needed repairs, find a tenant (or hire a property manager), and be the point person for any issues. As rent checks come in, you can pay the mortgage down and repay the investor's $20,000, and you split all the other proceeds 50/50. You own half the property and didn't put a dime of your own money into it! How great is that?

In all this, you aren't just investing in properties; you're investing in people, providing nice homes for families, helping grow communities, and creating jobs. Oh, and you're building wealth along the way.

Again, there is simply nothing in the world like real estate.

GREAT ... BUT NOT PERFECT

In this chapter, I just wanted to cover a handful of the major benefits of investing in real estate. Again, I love real estate, but it's not perfect. Like anything, real estate has plenty of pitfalls and a lot of things to account for. We'll get into the big ones in the following chapter, and I'll help you figure out if real estate could become an important piece of your financial pie.

CHAPTER 10

How to Get Started in Real Estate

My goal in the previous chapter was to introduce real estate investing to you as a strong, viable option for wealth building. Again, more people have become millionaires and billionaires through real estate than any other investing option, and for good reason: the tax system is structured to encourage private home-ownership and investing in properties. Now, does that mean real estate is right for everyone? Not necessarily. Now that I've gotten your attention about the perks of real estate, let's shift our focus to some of the risks that go along with those rewards. Then, I'll lay out a simple plan for starting your real estate investing journey.

RISKY BUSINESS

There are two main types of real estate investors: those who use debt and those who don't. The debt-free investor grows slowly using cash, maintaining a cycle of saving and buying. This kind of person wants to own the property outright from day one. This not only gives him a strong monthly cash flow position, it also enables him to sleep better at night. There's no chance of foreclosure, there's no big loan hanging over his head, and there's no panic if the property sits vacant for a few months. It's a fantastic way to go except for one thing: it's slow.

The investor who uses debt—usually either mortgages or loans from other investors—can grow much faster. But there are two trade-offs. First, debt cuts into your cash flow, as I'll discuss. Second, and more importantly for some, debt creates risk. And *more debt* creates *more risk*. If you start racking up three, seven, or fifteen different mortgages to fund your real estate deals, you could find your real estate adventure getting a bit more exciting than you expected. When a tenant gives notice that she'll be moving out, you might get nervous about being able to get another renter in there quickly to avoid interruptions in cash flow. Whenever you hear talk about a recession or rising unemployment, you'll have a little voice in the back of your mind asking how you're going to cover those mortgage payments if all your tenants lose their jobs.

If you aren't built to handle much risk, your real estate dream will give you nightmares every restless night. Absolutely every real estate investor I have known faces this at least once every fifteen or twenty years, and it's always harrowing. Most have survived each storm unless they are really up to their necks in debt without reserves. So, be thoughtful. It's like sailing or flying. Sunny days are fun, but stormy days are often a bit more than you wanted.

But these things don't just hit real estate investors; we see the same kind of cycles in something as "mundane" as a 401(k). The market goes up and the market goes down. Whichever market we're playing in, we have to be ready and willing to go for a ride. When the storm comes, we need to remember that it won't last forever. As I've said several times throughout this book, our job in tough times is to hang on and to look for the opportunities where others see only limitations. If you're going to have some sleepless nights, I'd rather you spend them dreaming about new, long-term opportunities instead of stressing about a short-term problem.

The most important lesson I've learned about real estate investing can be boiled down to two words: *know thyself*. You have to understand how you're wired and then match your real estate expectations to the level of risk you're comfortable with. Feeling a little nervous can be a good thing. It gets your blood pumping and motivates you to stay focused and work hard toward your goals. If you're crippled with fear and anxiety every time you open a mortgage statement, though, you're in too deep. You've violated the *know thyself* rule, and now you're paying the price. Your properties will never perform well enough to overcome a fundamental aversion to risk. If this is who you are, I suggest you either grow slowly with paid-for properties or set hard limits on how much debt or how many loans you can comfortably live with.

It's worth saying that almost nobody starts from scratch using cash. That takes an enormous amount of start-up capital, and most people aren't in the position to start writing house-sized checks. I've more commonly seen a risk-averse person start slowly with one mortgaged property. After she gets comfortable with how that property is performing, she might take a mortgage on a second. A couple of years later, she might take on a third. At that point, she might just stop and let those properties pay themselves off before going any further. By then, though, she may be comfortable enough to keep going. There's no right or wrong answer here. The only mistake would be for this investor to push herself further and faster than she is comfortable with. Trading your health, mental wellness, emotional stability, and peaceful sleep for a little bit of wealth is a horrible deal. No amount of money can buy these things back for you, so don't overextend your natural limits on risk. You'll just be trading misery for money.

On a personal note, I currently have mortgages on my large developments, but I am paying off my rental homes and smaller real estate deals similarly to how we talked about getting out of credit card debt earlier. I am choosing to pay off the small balances first.

My return on equity (my value after paying off the debt) will be lower but, as I get older, I am trading return for sleep.

That said, I also want to offer some encouragement to those who are comfortable with risk but still have something holding them back. A real estate developer friend once remarked, "There are only two types of properties: fully paid-off and fully mortgaged. There's nothing in between." He meant that paid-off properties are a breeze. No bank will ever bother you. Owning mortgaged properties, though, means the bank is in the driver's seat no matter how much or how little you owe. This is how I got slammed on the California housing development I discussed a few chapters back. They can foreclose on a $1,000 default just as surely as they can foreclose on a $100,000 or $10 million default. That's their right as the lender. However— and this is the point my friend was making—*banks don't want to own properties*. Once a bank starts the foreclosure process, they are facing a ticking clock called write-down to earnings and loan loss reserves. Their only goal is to not lose money or to lose as little money as possible. To accomplish this, they'll either work with you to get you back in good standing or they'll auction the house off to someone else as a foreclosure. Whichever option solves *their* problem (not yours) is the one they'll go with.

If you have a good relationship with your banker and a plan for how to make things right, the bank is less likely to foreclose because it will cost them a lot of time, trouble, and money. It's not because they're your friend; it's because they don't want to own your property. So, out of their selfish motivations, they'll work with you to get you back in good standing.

I've been the recipient of a few graces from banks over the years. Just this past year, the banks I work with called and gave me the option to make no payments on my loans for ninety days as part of the federal government's COVID-19 assistance plan. Why would the banks be so *generous*? It's not generosity! They just didn't want to deal with thousands of people calling to request special treatment during a national crisis. It was easier and cheaper for banks to let everyone skip payments for a few months than to deal with an endless stream of calls from panicked consumers.

My point here is that, even if you're an investor who uses debt to grow your portfolio, you aren't totally left all alone, twisting in the wind when things go south. The bank is motivated to help you, and the federal government has many protections in place to provide a safety net for people. I'm not saying this to convince you to outrun your risk tolerance but rather, to provide some context for those struggling to identify their individual comfort zones.

REAL ESTATE INCOME AND EXPENSES

Any investment comes with a mixed bag of income options and expenses, and real estate is certainly no different. In fact, real estate requires a bit more fine-tuning in the area of expenses because, unlike market-based securities, a house is a physical structure that requires maintenance and upkeep you don't have to worry about in other investments.

Aside from general maintenance and repairs, you'll have to plan for several little expenses that will stick their fingers in your real estate pie, such as:

- Homeowner's insurance
- Liability insurance
- Property taxes
- Vacancies (covering your expenses when the property isn't tenanted)
- Property management (the point person for leasing the property and dealing with the tenant)
- Homeowner's association dues (required in some neighborhoods and most condominiums)
- LLC fees
- Miscellaneous legal, accounting, and other professional services

In my experience, all these things amount to about three months' worth of rent. That leaves you with nine months of rental income to use to pay the mortgage, so be sure you're charging enough rent to cover everything without running negative every month.

Now, there have been times in my investing career when I've chosen to run negative cash flow on a property I wanted to purchase as a long-term investment, but those deals have been few and far between. More importantly, they have *always* been intentional. *Do not* miscalculate your income and expenses on a property and find yourself in the red every month. It can quickly turn your wealth-building efforts into a fast track to bankruptcy.

Of course, it's a different ball game if you pay cash for properties and skip the mortgage, because that leaves you with nine months of rental income per house after expenses. Paying cash for properties, though, means you're going to build much slower. As we've seen, that's the trade-off for the reduced risk.

On the income side, we've already seen how tax benefits, loan payoff, and appreciation work in our favor. And, of course, you can't forget about the monthly rent checks you have coming in from your tenants. This is all some investors are looking for. They have a dream of replacing the salary they earn at their job with passive income from monthly rent checks. There's nothing wrong with this strategy, and many people do it very effectively. The only real problem with this is that you need a *lot* of properties to hit the monthly cash flow required to leave your job. It can take a while to get there and, more importantly, it will usually require you to take on a fair amount of risk in the form of many mortgages while you wait for other people—your tenants—to pay off or at least pay down the mortgages on your properties so your equity goes up. By *equity*, I mean the value you have after you pay off any mortgage associated with your rental property. Some people have the stomach for risk; others do not. Remember, it's not the risk you wish you could take, it's what you can really handle. Be honest with yourself.

If your goal is to replace your income, do yourself a favor and run the numbers right now. Let's say you want to replace an income of $8,000 per month. How many houses would you need to own to get there? Assume your first property collects $2,000 in rent, and your mortgage payment is $1,200. Once you account for all the other little expenses, you might net $600 a month from that house until the loan is paid off. At that rate, you'd need *fourteen* houses to replace your income! I'm not trying to throw cold water on your dream, but you need to understand what you're looking at here. I'd love for you to own fourteen properties, but that's not going to happen overnight, especially with these numbers.

My strategy is different. I don't view my real estate investing as an escape from my nine-to-five existence. Rather, I view it as a long-term cash flow and net worth play. In the three decades I've been involved in real estate, I doubt I've pulled enough money out of my properties to buy myself a cup of Starbucks coffee. I prefer to view each property as a kind of building-shaped savings account. The rent is deposited into the account, and the mortgage and other expenses are auto-drafted out of the account every month. Once I have a new property up and running, I don't think about it very often. I know that if I just leave it alone, the rent will come in and the mortgage will be paid automatically month after month. Over time, the property will gradually pay itself off and go up in value. Occasionally, you can pull some retained earnings out of the house to buy more properties or make improvements to a property during a tenant turnover, so you can re-rent it for more rent. Aside from these reinvestments, I don't worry about it.

Later, when I retire, I'll have a portfolio of paid-off, cash-flowing properties that will be producing more than enough retirement income. I can use that money for my living expenses or to fund my retirement or I might keep doing what I've been doing all along—using the real estate income to purchase even more properties to increase my net worth and ultimately leave to my family or charities.

HOW TO START INVESTING IN REAL ESTATE

Again, it would be impossible for anyone to cover all the bases of real estate investing in a single chapter, but I want to be sure to give you *some* practical/tactical help for how to get started. Real estate is one of those activities that is best learned by *doing*, so the best thing you can do is get started and then find the mentors, partners, and investors you need to solve the problems and answer the questions that will inevitably pop up. So, here's my quick-action guide for getting started in real estate investing.

Step 1: Buy a Home to Live In

In most cases, the first property you buy should be your personal residence. The government highly incentivizes homeownership, and you can get some incredible financing deals and tax breaks as a first-time homebuyer. Those specific benefits aren't available to investors who won't be living in the home, and you probably will not be able to take advantage of the first-time homebuyer options on your personal residence later if you have already purchased investment properties. And even if you're not a first-time homebuyer, you'll get better financing options if you plan to live in the house you're buying since banks experience lower loan risk with homeowners than just about any other loan.

Now, there's a trick to this that you can take advantage of on every property you buy, even if you plan to turn them into rental properties. When you buy a property, plan to live there for a little while. If you intend to live there *at all*, you get the better financing and tax breaks that I've mentioned. But that doesn't mean you have to stay there forever. You could live there a year or two and then move out and rent the property to someone else. That way, you get all the incentives of a residential homebuyer *and* you still get to rent out the property.

This is an especially good way for someone who's young and single to get into the game. Buy a house, live there for six months or so while you plan your next deal, and then buy another one and move into it. If you live there for two years and then sell it, you may not have to pay taxes on the gains you make on the sale. There are exclusions on gains made on owner-occupied homes when sold. Even if you only buy houses that you will personally live in and never intend to rent out, you could buy a house every two years and make a huge tax-free profit on the sale each time. That alone could be an excellent little side hustle to someone who doesn't mind moving a lot.

Now, whether you're buying your first house as your personal residence or as an investment, *do not* buy a house until you are financially ready to do so. That means:

1. You're out of debt (except for maybe a car loan that you'll pay off within three years).
2. You have healthy savings of three to six months' of expenses (as we discussed in chapter 8).
3. You have a down payment of 20 percent *or* a plan to use multiple loans to borrow a 20 percent down payment. This enables you to avoid private mortgage insurance, which is expensive.

That last rule may sound a little weird if you aren't familiar with private mortgage insurance, better known as PMI. If you do not have at least 20 percent equity in your home at the time of purchase, the bank that issues your primary mortgage will require you to pay PMI, which is essentially a form of insurance that protects the bank (not you) if you default on your loan. Without a 20 percent down payment, you are considered at higher risk for defaulting and foreclosure, and the bank will put this protection in place to cover their costs if they need to foreclose on you. Basically, it means you're paying the bank's insurance premiums to protect them from you.

PMI is expensive, and it can be hard to get rid of once it's on your mortgage. My advice is to either save a 20 percent down payment outright or get a secondary loan to reach the 20 percent mark. For example, maybe you have 10 percent saved and you're ready to buy. You'd need a smaller loan for the other 10 percent you're missing, and that is totally separate from your primary mortgage. You're basically borrowing your down payment from one bank to pay the other. It's not an ideal situation, but it's worth it to avoid PMI.

In some cases, it doesn't make sense to buy a primary residence as your first home purchase. For example, maybe you're in the military and know you'll be moving every couple of years. In that case, it might make more sense to keep renting for yourself and buy an investment property as your first purchase.

Step 2: Get to Know Your Area

Real estate is local. Of course, you *can* buy properties anywhere in the country, but I strongly encourage you to stick close to home— at least until you know what you're doing. You want to be able to drive by the houses you own, even if you never do it.

I recommend buying a traditional single-family home in an average lower-middle-class neighborhood for your first investment property. The median price for this kind of home was $320,000 in 2020.[13] Real estate is all about location, though, so the figure will vary wildly depending on where you live. Do some research and see what the median price is in your town. Your goal will be to identify properties that are *one-third less* than the average-priced home. Those are the kinds of houses you'll want to buy. So, for easy math, let's say the average price in your area is $300,000. Your job is to target properties that are worth $200,000 (or as close as you can get to it).

Never, *ever* buy the top end of a community as an investment property. I can almost guarantee you will not get enough return on your money to make the deal worthwhile. If I could choose between the nicest home, the most average home, and the worst home in any neighborhood, I'd choose the worst one all day long. That gives you the chance to buy your way into a great neighborhood without breaking the bank. Plus, these homes are infinitely easier to rent than the nicest homes on the block. Why? Because the rent you'd need to charge on the nicest, most expensive home will outprice any reasonable renters looking for a place to live. You'll just attract people who can't afford to live there.

Let me show you how this strategy can work using a home I bought on Lake Tahoe many years ago. I found a house priced at $1.3 million literally on the same street as homes valued at more than $50 million. Was it ugly? Yes. Was it on the wrong side of the lake? Yes. Did it look like the Brady Bunch puked orange shag carpet all over the place? Absolutely. But so what? I renovated it, made it look nice, and flipped it for a $500,000 profit. Even after I updated everything, it was still the cheapest house on the street, but the buyer was thrilled to get something on Lake Tahoe at a price he could afford. He's lived there for thirteen years now, and that house has been a tremendous investment for him.

You may look at that and roll your eyes that I got that house for "only" $1.3 million, but I've done the same thing on regular family homes in your typical run-of-the-mill neighborhoods. I bought one for $30,000 in a neighborhood of $120,000 homes. It had a bad roof and holes in the flooring, reeked of cat pee, and had bad appliances. I spent $20,000 fixing it up. That plus the $30,000 I paid for the property put me at a total investment of $50,000. The improvements I made to the home, though, raised its value to over $100,000. I immediately rented it out for $850 a month, and it was consistently one of my best-performing rentals for many years.

Aiming at one-third less than average price will change the neighborhoods you're looking at. These will still be nice, safe areas, but they may be a little farther away from the heart of downtown and desirable attractions. The neighborhoods may be older than the newer, flashier areas, and the houses will have a little wear and tear. Do not let this scare you off. Remember, this is an investment property; it's not the house you're going to live in. You're buying it for *someone else* to live in, and that person will probably be a lot more excited about the home than you are.

Step 3: Find a Property That Meets the 10 Percent Rule

Once you identify some homes that cost a third less than the average home in the neighborhood, I want you to do a little more math and apply what I call the *10 Percent Rule*. That simply means your annual rent should total 10 percent of what you paid for the home. For example, say you purchase a home for $225,000. Ten percent of that is $22,500 per year, so you'd need to charge at least $1,875 per month in rent ($1,875/month x 12 months = $22,500). Knowing this, you can look for homes for sale in areas that can support that kind of rent payment.

Why 10 percent? Any less than that and you risk not making enough in rent to cover your mortgage and expenses and still generate free cash flow. If you ignore the 10 Percent Rule, the investment property you *thought* would be a good wealth-building tool has suddenly started taking money out of your pocket every month. I said earlier that there have been times when I've intentionally chosen to go cash flow negative on a property from time to time, but that is not a good strategy early in your investing career—and certainly not for your first property! Your first few properties need to be winners in terms of mortgage pay down and monthly cash flow. Otherwise, you'll get yourself in a bind early on that will take years to correct.

You might be surprised to learn it's a lot easier to meet the 10 Percent Rule on cheaper, smaller homes that aren't much to look at. Paying 25 percent more to buy a 25 percent nicer house does not mean you can rent it for 25 percent more money. You may get a few bucks more in rent for a $200,000 home than you would a $150,000 home, but it won't be 25 or 30 percent more. The best return on your money, in fact, is often on the least desirable homes. For example, I have friends who make a killing buying and renting manufactured homes. You can buy an older one for $15,000 that needs to be reconditioned, put a little money into fixing it up, and then rent it for $650 a month. You'd be making 40 percent on your money in that example! That's a lot better return than you'd get on a $200,000 home.

Of course, the appreciation isn't nearly as good on these, and you'll likely have more tenant issues and maintenance cost, but it's still a good example of the different kinds of strategies you can use to tailor your real estate investment to your interests and risk tolerance.

Step 4: Form an LLC

If you've done your work up to this point, you should have identified at least one property that checks all the boxes. But wait! It's not time to buy it yet! Before you buy the house, you need to define *who* is buying the house: you … or your investment company.

It is never a good idea to buy a rental property under your personal name. I'll let John Smith illustrate my point. John has a full-time job, a young family, a nice home, and some money in the bank. He is interested in real estate investing and decides to purchase a house down the street to rent out, so he makes an offer and buys it just like he bought his personal residence. Easy, right? Wrong. Here's the problem: a year later, his renter breaks her leg in her backyard, and she sues John for not taking care of some landscaping issues she said caused her to fall. Because John owns the rental property under his own name, his renter can now sue him for everything he owns—his personal home, his cars, his savings … *everything*. John really made a huge and expensive mistake.

Instead, he should have taken the extra step of forming an LLC—a limited liability company—before he purchased the investment property. By buying the property through an LLC, he could have protected his personal belongings from his renter and the lawsuit would have been limited to only what was owned by the LLC—which, in this case, was only the rental house. That's the sole purpose of an LLC: it limits liability. Without it, everything John and his family owns is at risk.

I cannot overstate how important this is. In fact, let's step out of the hypothetical and into a real-life example. A friend of mine, who works as a dentist, bought a home in Florida several years ago. His goal was to rent it out week to week as a vacation rental to pay off the mortgage, and then he planned to move into the paid-for Florida home when he retired. Since he ultimately planned to move into the home, he bought it in his own name. However, tragedy struck the very first month he owned the property. A toddler of one of his weekly renters drowned in the pool. Less than thirty days into his ownership, he was facing a multimillion-dollar lawsuit that put his dental practice and all his assets at risk. An LLC could have protected him from the far-reaching implications of that lawsuit, but it was too late. He spent the next year fighting to keep everything he and his family had. Remember, an ounce of prevention is worth a pound of cure.

Forming an LLC may sound intimidating, but it's a simple matter you can do on your own in a few hours and for very little money. You can hire a lawyer to help if you'd like to, or you could use online resources like LegalZoom, but it's not necessary. Just Google "how to form an LLC in [your state name]," and you'll find all the information you need, which will likely just be a link to the business section of your state's secretary of state website.

Step 5: Pull the Trigger

With your new LLC in place, you're ready to buy your first property. I'm often asked if new investors need to work with a real estate agent to identify and purchase properties, and my answer is yes and no. Using tools like Zillow and Redfin, most people can find properties that meet the criteria above. Real estate agents are almost exclusively trained to work with people looking for a place to live; they may not fully understand or respect the hard guidelines you put in place regarding buying one-third less than average and looking only at properties that meet the 10 Percent Rule. You could easily end up with an agent who shows you a dozen properties that don't come close to these criteria.

If you do want to work with an agent, though, I recommend finding someone who is new to the job and who doesn't yet have a lot of clients. This person will be more willing and able to spend time getting to know exactly what you're looking for and less likely to show you houses that are clearly outside your interests. Plus, it gives you the chance to build a relationship with an agent as you're both getting started. You have the opportunity to grow in the business together and the potential to do a lot of deals together over the next several years.

As for financing, your first deal will likely be with a plain-old conventional mortgage. It's a safe way to get started, and most people understand how they work (especially if they've already purchased their own home). If you go this route, I'd shop around for the best rate on a thirty-year mortgage for 80 percent of the home's value. The other 20 percent should come in the form of money you're bringing to closing, possibly combined with a smaller second loan as I discussed previously. If you have equity in your personal residence, you might consider using a home equity line of credit (HELOC) to fund your down payment on your investment property. Or, if you're lucky, you might already know someone with cash on hand who is looking to partner with you on a deal. That usually comes a little later in the game, but if you have that option, go for it. If you use a HELOC or an investor's money, though, make sure you pay that back first and as quickly as possible so you can shift your focus to paying off the regular mortgage.

Step 6: Rinse and Repeat!

Congratulations! You're a real estate investor! Now that you've got the ball rolling, you can grow your portfolio at your own pace, using income from your properties alongside loans and partnerships to finance new deals.

As you get more comfortable buying homes, I suggest you explore other types of properties. I have a special affinity for multifamily homes such as duplexes, triplexes, and even apartment buildings. Multifamily structures have lower appreciation, but the cash flow is generally much higher and per-tenant expenses are lower than single-family homes. For that reason, I encourage you to explore the multifamily options in your area.

You can get more creative over time in how you structure deals, too, especially as you gain a reputation for making good investments. This is where other investors come in. It's not uncommon for people with a lot of cash on hand to look for new places and ways to invest their money. You might meet someone with $300,000 to invest who is interested in real estate but doesn't have the time to do any of the work. If that were me, I'd use his money to buy ten different properties with $30,000 down payments on each, use the income to repay his investment first, and then split the ongoing profit with him. If or when we decide to sell the houses, we'd split that profit too.

In that kind of situation, how much of my money did I put into the deal? Zero! All I did was put in a little sweat equity, and I got to reap the reward of ten new investment properties! This may sound crazy to you, but it's the kind of thing I do every day. My deals are a lot bigger these days, of course, but this is how I started. You can't imagine how far that first rental property might take you one day!

OPTIONS APLENTY

Real estate is one of the most direct paths toward wealth building. It's insane how many things you have going for you when you take the plunge into real estate investing. You've got the federal government giving you tax incentives and savings that no one else gets. You've got inflation and appreciation driving your home value up and thereby increasing your net worth while you just sit back and watch. You've got low interest rates, making it easy and cheap to borrow money for property purchases. You've got investors who want the benefits of real estate with none of the effort who will line up to partner with you by funding your deals. You've got people in every city in the country looking for a good place to live. When you invest in real estate, you have all these things and more coming alongside you to help drive you toward your wealth goals.

Plus, real estate can be done with a very small investment, and it can be done with a very large investment. It can be done with tons of effort and experience, and it can be done in a total hands-off manner by working with others who have more time. There's simply no other investment class that comes close to the options, incentives, and benefits that real estate provides.

Does that mean you'll get rich quick? Absolutely not. There's no such thing as "get rich quick." There is, however, something called "get rich over time." You do that by being thoughtful and intentional, using the tools that are freely available to accelerate your wealth building and grow your financial pie. Like I said at the start of this chapter, real estate gives you more power than anything to build your financial pie over time. That doesn't necessarily mean that real estate is right for everyone, but it *is* a fantastic option for many, many people. Maybe even you.

CHAPTER 11

Stock Market Millionaire

I said in the previous chapter that most people understand real estate because they understand the nuances of buying, owning, and selling a physical structure. Not true with marketable securities like stocks, mutual funds, and index funds. These things are a lot more mysterious, primarily because it's hard for many people to understand what makes one company more valuable than another and why a company can lose value over something happening around the world in a seemingly unrelated fashion one day and rise in value for the same seemingly unrelated news the next. So let's start this discussion on the stock market by understanding where value comes from.

WHAT CREATES VALUE?

Before we talk about what creates value, you need to understand that public exchanges like stock markets provide liquidity and continual valuation based on supply and demand for the securities that trade on their market. These values move over the short term by many factors, including emotions. Imagine living next to a manic person who would sell you their house on a happy day for $300,000 and on a depressed day for $250,000. The person is setting the price based on their emotions, right? The stock market can seem to work the same way. Markets continually move from *undervalued* to *overvalued*. In fact, they are rarely *fairly* valued. That's where the fun comes in. With effort, you can begin to build tools that can help you discern where we are in the economic or a specific company's business cycle. Then the adage "buy low, sell high" comes into play. But first, let's talk about value.

All value in any area boils down to two things: supply and demand. Whether you're talking about real estate, consumer electronics, baseball cards, lawn care services, comic books, romantic partners, restaurants, or Fortune 500 companies, it all comes down to supply and demand. If you are selling a used iPhone and notice that Craigslist has hundreds of listings for similar phones in your area, it will have less value, meaning you'll have to price it lower than if you were in a small town with a limited supply of used iPhones. If you're a young guy on a college campus hoping to meet the girl of your dreams, and if your school has a 70:30 ratio of guys to girls, then those young ladies have much greater value than they'd have at a school with a 30:70 guy-to-girl split—only because the demand (men looking for women to date) is much greater than the supply (eligible women looking for a man to date). When the demand far exceeds the supply, value goes up. When the supply exceeds the demand, value goes down. It's really that simple.

The best example of this is real estate. Homes in San Diego, for example, will always be more valuable than homes in Macon, Georgia. Why? Because more people want to live in San Diego than Macon. The demand is higher. Now, you may absolutely love Macon. It could be your hometown, and you might not be able to imagine loving *any* city more than Macon. That's great! But that doesn't mean you can sell your family home in Macon for as much as you'd get for a similar home in San Diego. How you *feel* about your house and home-town is irrelevant. Feelings don't create financial value: supply and demand do.

Investing in marketable securities (the stock market) is no different. In fact, as I write this, we've just come through a global pandemic that changed the consumption patterns of the whole world. Business and vacation travel became nearly impossible, so the demand for airplane tickets and hotel rooms plummeted. Luxury resorts literally couldn't *give* rooms away because people weren't allowed to travel. Restaurants that were traditionally booked months in advance sat empty. You could park right at the front gate of Disney World, for crying out loud! For the first time in my life, all these wonderful things traditionally considered to be aspirational (if not impossible) luxuries were worthless. Out of nowhere, demand dropped to zero, taking the value of these services down the drain with it.

What else happened during the COVID-19 mess? People started working from home. This is something many businesses had slowly been inching into—or were dragged kicking and screaming into—for years. But then, without warning, the entire workforce was sent home. Services like Zoom, which most people had never heard of, suddenly became indispensable because all the employees at home needed a reliable way of videoconferencing with their remote coworkers. Sales of personal computers, long in decline, shot up because all those people needed computers to work on while they were working from home. Demand for these things exploded starting in March 2020, making them far more valuable than they were even a month earlier.

With all this in mind, what do you think happened to the stock prices of Delta Airlines and Marriott Hotels? They sank. Nobody needed what these companies provided, so their stocks—the market value of the company—dropped. At the same time, the stock price of Zoom (a video conferencing company) and Peloton (an interactive home workout system) shot up because the products and services these companies provide became immensely valuable. Bottom line: the demand for the products and services a company provides makes it more valuable or less valuable, and that value is measured in its stock price.

During that time, the market as a whole sold off substantially. The S&P 500 fell about 34 percent by March 23, 2020, meaning the average company dropped in value by about a third between mid-February and late March. Why? Because everybody was freaking out. Oil fell from over $60 a barrel to *negative* $40 a barrel. Oil producers literally had to *pay* someone to take oil as the majority of the world's oil containers were full to capacity. Investors driven by emotion panicked and sold their oil shares at the worst possible time—the bottom. Why? Because all we were hearing on the news was how horrible everything was. Newscasters declared it would take many years for oil to recover, that people would stay inside and stop driving, so there would be little demand for oil for a long time.

But what happened? The governments of the world reacted by pumping trillions of dollars into the financial system, which in turn began what will likely be viewed as the greatest buying opportunity of all time. We've talked about how wise people see the opportunity when others see only the limitation, right? That's exactly what smart investors did. They saw this for the incredible opportunity it was, and they bought a *lot* of oil stocks. It's important to set fear aside and realize that people are creatures of habit, and we all wanted to get back to normal as quickly as possible. Before long, demand returned and these equities came roaring back to life. But even then, the newscasters were warning people not to invest. They waited until oil had almost returned to $60 a barrel before they declared it "safe." That's crazy! In a nutshell, the so-called experts on TV were advising people to sell oil at the lowest price ever, then buy it again at its highest. That's exactly the opposite of what you want to do.

But if you understand the principles of supply and demand, you can use these events to get some once-in-a-lifetime deals. Maybe you can start to predict which companies will become more valuable or less valuable over time. You can ask yourself, *What's the demand for this product or service, and does Company ABC supply a better solution to meet that demand than Company XYZ does?*

You can even take this a step further by taking population data into account. There were 71.6 million baby boomers in America as of 2019, according to the US Census Bureau.[14] Boomers—the largest generation in history until recently—are in their late fifties to early seventies now. That's a huge consumer group. What do these people need? Senior housing. Medical care. Retirement communities. Smaller garden homes in warm climates like Florida. Self-storage. Demand for these things could become bigger than at any other point in history. So when you consider what to invest in or even *where* to invest, think about demographic trends and consumer habits.

Generation X accounts for 65.2 million people in their forties and early fifties.[15] This generation has kids in college. They're preparing for life as empty nesters. They're taking care of their aging parents. Their careers are in full swing. They might be a few years away from an inheritance from their boomer parents. How could the market demand created by this population impact my investing decisions? What companies might rise to meet that demand?

Millennials recently overtook boomers in size. There were 72.1 million millennials in their twenties and thirties in 2019.[16] They are just getting their careers off the ground. They're starting families. They grew up online. They're more mobile and less likely to buy a home than previous generations. They're more concerned with the environment and social issues. So what products and services might be in demand for this huge group? Personal electronics. Wedding resources. Childcare. Social media. Quality rental homes and apartments. Nightlife. Environmentally friendly options. If you can spot companies rising up to meet these demands, you could be at the forefront of a huge economic transfer as this generation takes over the workforce.

Good companies supply the needs today's marketplace demands. Great companies *anticipate* the demands of tomorrow and have a solution ready to go when the audience starts knocking. Like Wayne Gretzky famously said, "I skate to where the puck is going to be, not where it has been." Companies that do this go up in value. Investors who do this become millionaires by picking winners and riding them for the long term.

That's a basic primer on market value and the impact of supply and demand on a company's stock price. So . . . what do we *do* with that information?

HOW TO GET STARTED IN STOCK MARKET INVESTING

As with real estate, stock market investing comes in all shapes and sizes. There are dozens, maybe hundreds, of different ways to invest in the market. Some are fantastic, bringing returns you wouldn't believe. Some are OK, at least keeping your money ahead of inflation. Some are worse than the penny slots in the Las Vegas airport. As with anything else, the best option for you comes down to your personal comfort level with risk. Picking the right investments is all about risk, reward, and time line—basically, how long you have to wait and how much volatility you can endure. As we've seen elsewhere, the *know thyself* principle is key.

With that in mind, I want to suggest a practical strategy for you to get into market-based investing regardless of your financial situation, education, or experience in the stock market. There's no way I can cover *all* the options available to you, so I'll stick with four easy ones that cover the spectrum of risk.

Risk Level 1: Index Funds

Someone who is very risk-averse and, just as importantly, wants to get into the stock market as passively as possible without having to do any research whatsoever should start by buying into an index fund. With index funds and the other options I'm going to discuss here, I could give you the full-blown, Harvard-level, sophisticated explanation . . . or I could keep things simple and straightforward. Let's do the latter.

You've probably heard of the S&P 500 or NASDAQ. Even people who have no interest in the stock market hear these terms thrown around on the news when the market tanks. For example, you may hear that the S&P 500 dropped X number of points in a single day. Even if you don't know what that means, the news anchor's tone of voice lets you know it's a bad thing. But what is the S&P 500? Simple: it's an index that includes a mix of five hundred fairly large companies. It's not the five hundred biggest companies; it's just five hundred businesses that cover the gamut of American industries. Some names you'd know that are in the S&P are Apple, Tesla, Southwest Airlines, American Express, CarMax, General Mills, The Home Depot, Coca-Cola, Pfizer, AT&T, and Visa. You'll notice that these companies all do different things. That's because the S&P 500 includes eleven different sectors representing various industries. Sectors include things like communication services, energy, financials, technology, and healthcare.

So, here's what the S&P 500 index does: It gives us a little window into how the stock market *as a whole* is doing. Because the S&P represents all different types of companies across all different types of industries, the day-to-day performance of the S&P shows us how the American economy is doing overall. If the S&P is up, it means most companies and industries are having a good day. If it's down, it means consumers and investors are jittery and taking their money out of the market for some reason. That brings the economy—and the stock market—down temporarily.

It's important to note that this list of five hundred companies isn't set in stone. In fact, companies come and go from the S&P 500 all the time to keep up with the needs of modern consumers. Eighty years ago, you'd have found telegraph and radio broadcast companies on the list in the communications sector. Today, you'll find AT&T, Verizon, Fox, and Comcast there instead. Horse-drawn buggies aren't a good economic metric anymore, but Tesla and Ford are. These are dramatic examples, of course, but you get the point. The companies in the S&P 500 change to keep up with the times.

It's also important to know that the companies in the index are not weighted equally. Bigger businesses—those that represent more wealth—have a tremendous impact on the S&P 500 value, while smaller companies have a negligible impact. In fact, the 10 largest companies (Apple, Microsoft, Amazon, Facebook, etc.) account for more than 27 percent of the market capitalization of the index. The top 50 companies drive most of the index's value, pulling the other 450 companies with it. So if Apple has a good day and Hewlett Packard (HP) has a bad day, it's not the end of the world. That's because Apple's "weight" on the index is literally one hundred times greater than HP!

Another index you've probably heard of, NASDAQ, works the same way as the S&P 500, but NASDAQ is more focused on the technology sector and emerging growth companies. It's less of an overall look across *every* industry and is more representative of a handful of key growth areas that help drive the economy.

So, how does this quick lesson on indexes help a typical investor who wants to get started in the market but doesn't want to spend much time learning this stuff? Easy: You can simply buy an index fund. Rather than buying stock in a single company, you can basically buy a piece of the *entire* S&P 500 or NASDAQ indexes. This provides lower company-specific risk because you aren't betting the farm on any one company. Instead, you're betting on the entire US economy (S&P 500) or on one huge sector of the economy, like technology (NASDAQ). The rate of return on an index fund isn't as *great* as it could be if you pick a huge winner, but it's a diversified way to have exposure across a wide group of companies at a very low fee. In fact, the great majority of mutual funds do not perform as well as the indexes do over time. It's at least good enough to keep your money growing over time and likely ahead of inflation. And fees are incredibly low with index funds, meaning your earnings won't be eaten up by a ton of nickel-and-dime fees.

In my opinion, index funds are the very definition of diversified, broad economic investing. It can even make you wealthy over a long period of time. And, as I've said, if you believe the US economy will grow over time, put more money in when everyone else is being scared away. Those are usually the best times to get a deal. I once heard someone say, "You pay a really high price for a rosy outlook." That is, if everyone is excited about a particular investment, you've probably already missed your chance to get a great deal.

Risk Level 2: Exchange-Traded Funds

If you want to take a little more risk in exchange for a little more (potential) reward, you can invest in an exchange-traded fund, or ETF. An ETF is traded on a stock exchange like a regular single stock, but it acts more like an index fund. The difference between an ETF and an index fund, though, is that an ETF can be structured around a more specific set of companies, sectors, or industries. For example, instead of buying an index fund that represents the entire S&P 500, I could buy an ETF that focuses exclusively on the travel sector. Why might this be a good idea? Well, think about what happened to the travel industry right after 9/11 or the COVID-19 pandemic. As I've said, the hotel, airline, and tourism industries tanked—*temporarily*. But what always happens after events like these? The industry springs back to life, often bigger and better than ever! So, in the spirit of looking for opportunity when others see limits, you could have purchased an ETF focused on a handful of companies in the travel industry when the market dipped in that sector. Then, you get to ride the rebound as the industry recovers without ever having to research any travel-related companies. You simply concluded that travel is down due to COVID-19, but you're pretty sure it'll come back. So, you focus on the travel sector. The same can be done in many sectors. That's how I approached the drop in oil that I mentioned earlier.

Newer ETFs, like blockchain and cloud computing, can give investors returns focused on an area that is currently growing very quickly. Obviously, companies like Google, Amazon, Facebook, and Netflix are currently growing in importance and market value, but it's fun to look and learn what's on the horizon. It's hard to imagine a situation in which technology as a whole suddenly falls apart over the next ten or twenty years, so I like putting my money into areas of high demand that solve problems or somehow make life easier. And, more so than index funds, ETFs give me the chance to put money in areas that I like by narrowing my focus into smaller slices of the greater market.

ETFs are fairly easy to manage, have slightly higher fees and more risk than index funds, and offer the potential for greater rewards. And, because your investment is spread across a number of different companies (as with index funds), you still get the benefit of diversification. This gives you some protection if one of the companies in the ETF implodes for some reason.

Risk Level 3: Mutual Funds

If you want to kick things up a notch and have an active manager, you can get into mutual funds. In fact, if you participate in your company's 401(k) plan, you're probably *already* investing in mutual funds. That's commonly the type of investment you'll find in a company's 401(k).

A mutual fund represents the next stage of investment as we narrow our scope from index funds (investing in an entire index like the S&P 500) to an ETF (investing in a sector of the market) and now to mutual funds. A mutual fund is a mix of several companies rolled together not by sector but by the style of investing. You could invest in small capitalization growth stock mutual funds, for example, which represent a collection of companies that are just emerging and/or are expected to enter a period of growth that will outpace the overall market. Or you could go with large growth mutual funds, which represent fairly stable, maybe even "boring" companies with a good track record of growth over time. There are international mutual funds, which represent companies outside the United States. There are aggressive growth mutual funds, which represent companies with huge growth potential but carry a high level of risk because they're unproven. In all of these, you can see how the specific sector or industry isn't the focus but instead the attention is placed on the growth rate of the companies within the fund and the investing strategy of the individual investor.

You absolutely can build wealth by sticking just with mutual funds. Before you get this far, though, I strongly encourage you to work with a professional advisor to customize your investing goals and identify the best mutual funds, ETFs, or index funds to help you get where you want to go.

Risk Level 4: Single Stocks

The highest-risk, highest-potential-reward option is the traditional single stock. The risk is high on this one because you're stripping away all the diversification that helped protect you in index funds, ETFs, and mutual funds. When you buy a single stock, you're buying a little piece of *one* company. Just one. If that company's stock goes up in value, you make money. If it goes down, you lose money. Period. You are literally betting your money on one horse. No matter what the company is or how long they've been around, it's still one company.

That said, I personally invest in single stocks all the time. I've had some enormous winners, and I've had my share of painful losses. Anyone who's been investing for a while has ridden that same roller coaster a few times. The only way to properly diversify in single stocks is to create your own diversification by building a portfolio of stocks that you own. You can pick whatever companies in whatever sectors you want. The idea is to create a portfolio of multiple stocks across multiple industries. That way you can hopefully mitigate your losses in one company with your gains in the others.

Every investor goes about this differently, so you'll need to work with a professional advisor to get started and to craft a personalized plan that works for you. Many advisors work only with mutual funds, index funds, and ETFs, but there are advisors who do work with single-stock strategies.

Personally, as I've said, I like the technology sector. My preference is to invest in companies that are primed for rapid growth, and nothing rings that bell for me more than technology right now. So I might invest in Apple, Roku, Amazon, Microsoft, Alphabet (Google's parent company), and OKTA Networks. *Please note this is not a recommendation for anyone else to buy these! Talk to your own investment advisor.* It's obvious that artificial intelligence, electric vehicles, battery technology, and biotech—just to name a few—are likely to experience massive growth in the future. It's your job to see the big changes and then do a little work trying to identify how to invest in leading companies in massive growth sectors. I'd also keep my eyes open for brand-new emerging industries that haven't hit it big yet but I think probably will. That's likely the riskiest bet you can take in single stocks. When it works, the payoff can be huge. But when it doesn't, the losses can be heartbreaking.

One strategy I've seen work for many investors is to start by looking at the individual companies inside an ETF, identifying which ones are growing the fastest, and then buying just those individual companies' stock. Sometimes an investor will feel a personal affinity for a company—like a longtime fan of Disney's movies and amusement parks—and buy that company's stock as a next step in their "relationship" with the brand. If you buy every product and service a company offers, it only makes sense that you'd want to own a tiny piece of the company itself through a stock purchase. There's nothing wrong with that, but don't let emotion and brand loyalty drive your investing decisions. Always keep a critical eye on the bottom line. We'll talk more about that in this chapter.

Single stock investing can be a wild ride—one that can make you or break you. Do not—I repeat, *do not*—go into this blindly. Educate yourself on the market and individual companies before you put a dime into single stocks. Fortunately, there are many wonderful online resources that can help you identify companies that are either growing or are primed for growth in the near future. One of my favorite sites for buy and sell recommendations is The Motley Fool (www.fool.com). If you don't do anything else, at least comb through their great educational materials before you make a move into single stocks.

HOW TO (HOPEFULLY) PICK WINNERS

When evaluating companies as potential investments, the first thing to know is that there are no guarantees. None. At all. You never know with 100 percent certainty what's going to happen tomorrow and how that news or event will impact a company's stock price. A company can do everything right and still get caught in an unexpected whirlwind of negative factors outside their control that takes them out.

And, of course, there are companies that you *think* are doing everything right when they're actually days away from a scandal that will blow the doors off the place. Remember Enron? That was once perceived as one of the safest bets investors could make ... until the news broke that the entire company was built on a house of cards and lies. The company imploded, the stock price went to zero, and thousands of people saw their retirement savings evaporate overnight. Theranos is another, more recent example. This medical testing company and its Steve Jobs–like founder was the darling of the tech and investing world for a couple of years ... until a handful of whistleblowers inside the company sounded the alarm that the technology the entire company was built around didn't exist. The whole thing was a scam. Anyone who put money into Theranos lost it. Many investors lost their reputations as well.

I'm not trying to scare you; I'm just trying to make it crystal clear that nobody can make any foolproof guarantees about a company or a stock. Not me, not your advisor, not the analysts on the news. The best you can do is to do your research, work with people with a good track record, and never invest more money than you can afford to lose. If you have $10,000 to invest, and if that $10,000 is the only thing standing between you and bankruptcy, don't bet all that money on one horse, no matter how good that horse looks.

The second thing to watch out for is emotion. The stock market can be volatile, but it's not emotional. You have to take emotion— things like fear, greed, herd mentality, the "greater fool theory" (the idea that you can always sell overpriced securities to a "greater fool"), and affection for a particular brand—out of it. Look at things rationally and remember our quick study on supply and demand. If you want to find winning stocks, the goal is to invest your money in companies that are supplying the things people want and need *when* they want and need them. In rental real estate, I reminded you that you aren't buying a house that *you'll* live in. With stocks, I'll remind you that you aren't necessarily buying stock in companies that *you'll* use or enjoy. If enough other people are buying their products, it doesn't matter if you do. You might hate iPhones and MacBooks, but you can still potentially build wealth with Apple's stock. Even that is no sure thing, though. Apple has grown like crazy over the last decade, but as the old saying goes, "previous results are no guarantee of future results."

Watch the Trends

Using Gretzky's "skate to where the puck is going to be" mentality, how can we look at the marketplace and identify companies that are on the cusp of breaking through to the big time? The number-one method is to train yourself to watch for trends. As the father of five, I believe the one overlooked way to watch trend trajectory is to look at what your kids are doing. Remember the huge impact demographics has on consumption. For some reason, many people overlook the combined spending power of kids, who greatly influence their parents' spending. As such, teenagers have an unbelievable impact on the current and future value of a company's stock price. I'm sure you've noticed that by the time people in their thirties and forties catch on to what's "cool," that product or service is already on the way out. Facebook is a great example of this. There are basically no kids on Facebook anymore. It started as a service exclusively for college students before opening up to younger teens and everyone else. Kids and young adults flocked to the service and absolutely loved it . . . until their parents started signing up. Once people my age started commenting on our kids' status updates, they were gone. Facebook lost its cool factor, and the young crowd moved to Instagram.

At this point, Facebook made a genius move: they bought Instagram but kept the two brands separate. That way Facebook's aging brand reputation didn't tarnish Instagram's public persona as the hot new thing for young adults. Without that move, I don't think Facebook's stock would have performed so well since the acquisition. But because they showed some shrewd awareness of how to keep their value high while the trends changed around them, Facebook remains a strong player in the market.

Once you start looking, you can see changing trends everywhere. Because I like tech stocks, I've been especially interested in the 5G cellular rollout of the past couple of years. This is a major shift in how cell companies work, and faster 5G service will open many new doors for typical consumers, especially those who don't have high-speed internet services at home. Third World countries can skip the physical infrastructure of traditional cable and telephone networks and catch up almost overnight from a technology, information, and communication perspective. Think of the educational opportunities this opens up and how consumption patterns will be affected by greater access to social media and brand influencers.

You might look at 5G and think that the only ones benefiting are the carriers like Verizon and T-Mobile, but that's not true at all. This one changing trend is opening up new opportunities for count-less companies and industries, such as the companies who build the cell towers, phone manufactures like Apple and Samsung, and chip manufacturers like Qualcomm, which makes the antennas for most of the phones on the market. And, of course, every web-based company benefits when more people get better access to the internet, so companies like Google and Amazon will no doubt gain many more users and customers. Think of securing and storing all the data that will be stored in the cloud. I can go on and on, but every material change is like throwing a big rock in a pond: all you have to do is anticipate the ripples and invest before the wave hits. Because I keep my eye on changing technologies and seek to understand how it might impact the market, I've been able to jump into several tech stocks before they really took off. It's not really luck, and it certainly isn't magic. It's just a matter of paying attention to trends.

Look Where Growth Is Happening

Think about how our shopping has changed. When I was at an investment bank many years ago, our investment banking team backed out of a company I thought had some potential. The decision-makers said, "Who would invest in an online yard sale company?" That company was eBay. Many said the same thing about a little online bookstore: "It won't work. People like to hold a book in their hands and scan through it before they buy." That company was Amazon. Others saw new start-ups and said, "Who wants to ride in a random person's car or sleep in a stranger's house?" Those companies were Uber and Airbnb.

Today, the world's largest retailer has practically no physical stores. The world's largest transportation company has no fleet of its own. And the seller of more places to sleep doesn't even own a bed. Look for that kind of transformational change with huge market potential or for new companies disrupting entire markets. Those could be tomorrow's big winners. For example, I've mentioned owning a Tesla several times in this book as an aspirational goal. Why do you think this brand name—a name no one had even heard of fifteen years ago—has become such a major status symbol of wealth for people today?

Tesla's founder, Elon Musk, launched a brand-new car company in the twenty-first century that's going toe-to-toe with the likes of Ford, Mercedes, BMW, Lexus, and Infinity. How? Because he rose to meet a rising demand—electric vehicles—that the other manufacturers weren't taking seriously. There hadn't been any significant advancements in car design and engineering in decades before Musk exploded onto the car scene like an atom bomb. Now, less than twenty years later, the biggest names in the industry are scrambling to catch up to Tesla in technology, reputation, and market value. And, in the process, Elon Musk became one of the richest people in the world.

Remember, it's all about supply and demand. When an upstart rises to meet the demands of a large sector, pay attention—particularly if they have a visionary leader and are trying to disrupt a technology or process. Musk didn't *just* change car technologies, after all. He disrupted the way car companies *sold* cars by requiring only one signature, bypassing traditional dealerships that would add to the cost, pushing model and option selection back on the customer, updating the car's software and even adding features through software updates, and building a nationwide charging network. All the other manufacturers thought he was crazy. But now, Tesla sells more midsized luxury cars than all the others, and they will soon have the highest profit margins in the industry. People are blinded by familiarity, so they often don't recognize the value of change. But today's ideas don't fit in yesterday's containers. Elon Musk isn't concerned with *what was*. He's focused on *what can be*. And that's creating massive value.

But Musk isn't the only one making these kinds of moves. You might be watching the next Tesla-type company appear right before your eyes. You could buy stock in a company the day they make their IPO (initial public offering) that could make you a millionaire.

Look at the Numbers

You also need to take a good look at a company's financials. You can't always go by a company's reputation or popularity. At the end of the day, if a company burns through all their cash, they won't stay in business long. A business on the verge of bankruptcy is probably not going to be a good long-term stock investment for you.

And don't just look at their sales figures. It's easy to be swayed by what appears to be massive sales numbers, but sales don't tell the whole story. In fact, sales don't even tell the most important part of the story. I'm more interested in a company's net income or path to income and free cash flow. In layman's terms, *net income* is simply revenue minus expenses. It's what's left over after a business pays all their bills. Oftentimes you'll find a company with impressive sales figures but terrible net profits. That tells me their profit margin is way too slim to be successful long term. There are some exceptions where fast-growing companies need to reach hundreds of millions or even billions in revenues before they break even if they have significant fixed costs associated with getting the business up and running. Once they break even and those fixed costs are covered, though, the business may have relatively small variable costs moving forward. That could cause an explosion in profits, which in turn would likely drive their value up.

For example, a widget company that sells a million widgets at $100 apiece may look good at first glance. If it *costs* them $90 to manufacture each widget, though, they're making only one-tenth the money their sales figures show. And Lord help them if it costs them $110 to make each widget. That means they're *losing* ten bucks per sale. This is the kind of detail you get only by taking a good look at the *entire* financial picture.

This emphasis on net profit is one thing that makes Apple such an impressive business. Sure, Apple makes a ton of money in sales, but the most impressive thing about them is how much *profit* they make per sale. CEO Tim Cook is a master of squeezing every last penny out of the supply chain, giving Apple incredible—maybe even unprecedented—profit margins on their products. It costs an estimated $490 in parts for Apple to produce an iPhone it can sell for up to $1,400. With that kind of spread, plus their more recent entry into online services and cloud storage subscriptions, it's little wonder why Apple is one of the most-valued companies on the market today.

HOW MOST PEOPLE SCREW UP

The financial industry—stock investing in particular—is the only industry I've ever seen where people hate to buy things on sale. People love to pay full price for stocks. Now, they may not *say* that, but most investors *act* like it.

A few years ago, you couldn't *give away* Tesla stock when it was trading for $300 per share. Then, in August of 2018, Elon Musk said some crazy things on Twitter that got him in trouble with the SEC, joking about how he had secured funding to take Tesla private at $420 per share. The "420" was a goofy reference to pot, apparently one of Musk's forms of relaxation. Tesla shares were trading at around $340 at the time, then shot up to $390 after his now-infamous tweet. The following year, production delays hit Tesla hard, and the stock fell to under $200 by summer of 2019.[17] If you were looking for a sale on Tesla stock, that was it. By the end of that year, the company rallied and had shot up past $400. By New Year's Day 2020, Tesla was closing in on $500 per share. As I sit here writing this, Tesla is trading at an astounding $617.

But wait, it gets even better; the current $617 doesn't tell the whole story. When Tesla hit $3,000 in August of 2020, the stock split 5:1, meaning investors were given five shares at $600 rather than one share at $3,000. So, when you account for the split, the value of Tesla's stock went from $200 to $3,000 in just a couple of years. Today, people are flocking to Tesla at its highest price. Wall Street loves the company now, but where were they when the darn thing was on sale for $200? In fact, some of the supposedly "smart" hedge fund managers were betting against Musk by selling his stock short, a position where you make money if the stock goes down and conversely lose money if the stock goes up. These investors acted so smart and appeared on financial shows to express their genius at selling short. When the stock ran up many times over, though, Musk had the last laugh. He mailed pairs of shorts to their homes as a joke. I really like that guy and his resolve to win.

The Biggest, Most Common Mistake

That brings me to the biggest mistake people make when it comes to investing in marketable securities: they buy and sell *at the exact wrong time*. And when I say *they*, I really mean *we*—because I've done it too. When this little online bookstore called Amazon went public, I had a hunch it would change the world. I bought shares of Amazon not long after their IPO in May 1997. If I had held that stock, it'd be worth well over $100 million today. And by well over, I mean *well over*. But I didn't hold it. I sold it in 2000 during the dot-com bust and bought some unimproved land. Why did I sell Amazon? It made sense at the time. They hadn't made a profit yet, and the founder was saying some crazy things about his views on growing the company. NASDAQ went down almost 90 percent, I freaked out, and I sold many of my tech stocks—including Amazon.

That one boneheaded decision cost me well over $100 million! Sadly, that wasn't the only time I screwed up. I also missed out on more than $100 million by selling my Qualcomm stock at the wrong time. And I bought Home Depot in the 1980s and sold it before it became a household name. Oh, did I mention Cisco, Microsoft, Oracle, and eBay? I've owned and sold them all. All told, I've missed out on hundreds of millions in gains simply by selling stocks at the wrong time.

Why do we buy and sell at the wrong time? People are more reactive than proactive. We see something happening and *then* start taking action. We don't think about buying an umbrella until *after* it starts raining. We don't buy a stock until the price has already gone up. We sell when the price drops instead of backing up the truck and buying more or holding on for the ride. We get scared, and we react out of fear. It's human nature. We start with $400,000 and watch it drop to $280,000. We freak out and think, *I've got to get out of this before I lose everything!* The problem is, we sell at the bottom and completely miss out on the recovery. Think about all the people who bought Tesla in the $300s and then panicked and sold it all at $200 when it bottomed out. How many more millionaires would we have in this country if those people had just held on, tempered their fear, and committed to riding things out?

The market drops. You can absolutely count on it. There will be days when your favorite stock looks like it's falling apart. You might wake up one morning and realize you've "lost" thousands or maybe hundreds of thousands overnight. But here's the thing: you really haven't. It looks like you have on paper, but that's all it is—a *paper loss*. It doesn't change your bank account. You don't suddenly *owe* money to anyone. A piece of paper you own is just worth less today than it was yesterday, meaning you'd get less for it today *if you sold it*. But you don't have to sell it. The only way to actually lose money during a market drop is if you sell your stock. The loss isn't *real* until the moment you sell. At that point, yes, it's a loss. Like financial radio host Dave Ramsey says, "The only people who get hurt on a roller coaster are the ones who jump off." But if you hold the stock, you get to participate in the recovery. You get to ride the roller coaster back up the hill, maybe higher than it's ever been.

At this point in my investing career, I've learned not to panic, at least for the most part, when my stocks take a dip. In fact, in the times I once felt compelled to sell out of fear, I now do just the opposite: I buy. If it's a stock I still believe in, even if it's having a bad day, I might double down on it. Instead of selling all my stock and realizing the loss, I'll think of it like a sale and buy more. I'm doing that right now, in fact. I own a bunch of Roku stock, and they've been in a public spat with Google for the past couple of months as I write this. Their price has bounced around day to day as a result, but I still believe in Roku as one of the leaders in digital content delivery moving forward. So, instead of selling all my Roku stock in a panic this month, I've actually bought more. Why shouldn't I? One of my favorite products is on sale, so it's a good time to stock up.

When SHOULD You Sell?

Warren Buffett has joked that every investor should get a punch card with twenty-five investment decisions for life. That is, he thinks investors should make as few selling decisions as possible over the course of their investing career. The time and emphasis should be put on the front end, on the purchase. Buying a stock is serious business, a decision that shouldn't be taken lightly. You should treat a stock purchase like a marriage of sorts: you're committing yourself to it— in good times and bad, in sickness and in health, for better and for worse. When you have this mindset in your investing, you free yourself from the allure of fear-driven selling at the worst possible time. Hopefully, you wouldn't leave your spouse after one particularly bad day or week. You shouldn't leave your stocks that way either. If you aren't mentally and emotionally prepared to commit to a stock for the long haul, you shouldn't buy it in the first place. Stick to index funds or mutual funds.

That said, there are certainly situations in single stocks when it's time to cut and run. But take the emotion out of it by applying a hard guideline beforehand. For me, I'm inclined to sell a single stock if the company misses earnings two quarters in a row. I don't worry about a single down quarter, but two in a row can indicate the start of a downward spiral. If something you own is missing their own expected earnings, it's time to see if it's a company-specific issue or an industry-specific issue. If it's company-specific, it's time to consider getting out.

You don't have to, of course. Even then, you might still choose to hang on, ride it out, and accept whatever happens, good or bad. I have a friend, for example, who never sells anything he buys. Never. He regularly buys $10,000 of different companies' stock, and he holds it forever, no matter what. When he spends that $10,000, he emotionally disconnects from it, freeing it up to do its job. Playing this strategy, he's had many, many losses. But guess what? He's also had some huge wins—and the wins have more than made up for his losses. Just by applying this strategy, buying stocks that interest him in $10,000 blocks and never selling, he's averaged a 15 percent return per year—beating the market average by about 50 percent. It's an interesting approach because it removes the biggest danger in single-stock investing: selling at the wrong time. He can invest for fun and never stress about "timing the market," because selling isn't an option. Now, this isn't what I do myself, but I can definitely see the advantages of it. And I can't argue with his returns!

STOCK MARKET VS.
OTHER INVESTING OPTIONS

So far in this book, we've covered several different kinds of investing options, such as 401(k), Roth IRA, and real estate. Now, in this chapter, we've added marketable securities such as index funds, exchange-traded funds, mutual funds, and single stocks. At this point, you might be asking, "Why would I want to get into securities instead of just doing all my investing in my 401(k)?" That's a good question, and I'll answer it briefly: There's no need to move beyond your 401(k) and other "easy" retirement plan options *unless you're trying to take investing seriously and amass additional wealth over time.* Once you are used to investing and not spending all you make, you can see very significant changes in your net worth. In fact, my first $1 million account when I was starting as a financial consultant in the late 1980s was a waitress at Red Lobster who, through stock picking, had grown her investment portfolio to over $1 million by investing in companies she liked. Building wealth isn't about *easy*; it's about persistence and discipline over time.

Retirement accounts will always be easier, whether you're using company-sponsored plans like a 401(k) or do-it-yourself options like a Roth IRA. These things have a "set it and forget it" simplicity. You can even set up contributions to come directly out of your paycheck so you never even have to think about it. You can put your entire retirement plan on autopilot and get on with your life. If that's what you want to do, go for it. As long as you start early and contribute throughout your working years, you'll probably be fine and have a comfortable retirement. You'll probably even become a millionaire by the time you retire. Listen, that's great. That's more than most people are doing. If you get to age sixty-five with $2 or $3 million in your IRA, you're going to be fine.

But . . .

There's a big *but* here, and it should be obvious: if you want to make many times more than that, if you want to build wealth in the eight or nine figures, and if you want to do it before your sixties, you've got to think past your retirement accounts. You can't even withdraw any money without penalties from an IRA until you're almost sixty, so having $2 million in the IRA doesn't do anything for your lifestyle in your thirties, forties, and fifties. You'd just have a pile of money you can't touch yet. And even under the best circumstances, there's no reality in which you can build up $100 million in an IRA. No chance. That kind of wealth happens only when you kick things up a notch, take greater risk, and play a more active role in your wealth building. And that's usually done at least partially through securities.

Of course, as we saw in the previous chapter, you can also build a pile of wealth in real estate, and that remains the number-one way people become millionaires. I've explained how much I love real estate, but I want to be honest here: real estate is a better option only because of all the special tax treatment and incentives the government gives real estate owners and investors. If those incentives went away, I would never buy another property.

As much money as I've made from it, real estate is a pain in the butt compared to the stock market. I can buy a house for $10,000–$25,000 out of pocket and borrow the difference. Then, I have to deal with a mortgage or investors. I have to work to pay it off over time. I deal with leasing, selling, commissions, and property management. I have to put up with difficult tenants. I face the occasional eviction. And I do it all for maybe a 15–20 percent return per year on my equity. Compare that to what I can do with the same $10,000–$25,000 in the stock market. I can invest that money in a tech stock in a growing market. I get the benefit of thousands of employees working hard every day to make that company more valuable. The company has unlimited growth potential and a global market of customers. Companies like Amazon, Berkshire Hathaway, Walmart, The Home Depot, Microsoft, and Cisco have all created many millionaires. Owning great companies in growing markets with excellent management often yields returns that are very unlikely elsewhere, and you don't have to do anything except put in that initial $10,000 investment. No tenants. No property managers. No yardwork. Nothing. And if you left that stock alone as it grew for twenty years, you could likely outperform most other investment types. You wouldn't have $2 or $3 million; you could have more like $10 million or more, all from that one $10,000 investment. Of course—and I want to be crystal clear here—this is much easier said than done. But it *has* happened. And it will happen again.

These are the kinds of numbers that, although unlikely, are possible if you get in early on an Amazon, Tesla, Roku, or Nvidia. I'm not talking about getting to the point of being "comfortable" in retirement; I'm talking about someone with an average income becoming a multi-multimillionaire! Now, it's a long shot to get that kind of return, but what if you only did *half* as good? That's still pretty incredible! As I write this, PayPal's ten-year return is just over 23 percent. If you had bought $10,000 worth of PayPal in 2011, when it was already a household name, you would have nearly $100,000 by 2021. Or take a company as "boring" as Costco. It's averaged a little over 20 percent over the past decade. In that time frame, your $10,000 would have grown to over $76,000.

Or, what if you, like my friend, simply bought growth companies and left them alone to do what they will do? Who knows what could happen? Like Einstein said, compound return is the eighth wonder of the world! You can buy stock with very little investment using an online brokerage service like E*TRADE or Robinhood. Many services have educational tools as well.

Yes, you should participate in retirement savings programs and take advantage of opportunities like a company match and tax-free growth in a Roth IRA. We talked about those things in chapter 8. And yes, you should check out real estate and see how you can use the tax code to your advantage by investing in properties as we discussed in chapter 9. Those things can and will make you rich over time, but don't stop there! Keep pushing, keep going, keep growing as you expand your wealth building into the stock market. There is *serious* money there, and it's yours for the making. And, along the way, you get to participate in the single biggest economic engine in world history: the American economy.

I never want people to invest in things they don't understand or aren't comfortable with. That's why I've given you a spectrum of options in this chapter, from index funds to single stocks, to help you get started in the stock market. Don't go crazy right out of the gate, and never take on more risk than you can stomach. But do *something*. There are more than 20 million millionaires in the United States today, and most of them are people just like you: regular men and women with regular jobs who decided they wanted more than just a paycheck-to-paycheck existence. They wanted wealth. Heck, they wanted to be *rich*! And now they are. They did it, and so can you.

But it requires a decision, a deliberate choice to put your key into the economic engine of America. We'll talk about what that decision looks like in the final chapter.

CHAPTER 12

Four Choices
for Success

I *mpact.*
Everything we've talked about in this book—every goal, hope, dream, and aspiration—comes down to the *impact* we want to have on the world around us. We want to matter. We want to make a difference. We want to leave a legacy of love, wisdom, encouragement, and, yes, *money* when we're gone. That's something that drives every millionaire I've known throughout my career: we all want to live and work in such a way that we make the world a better place, both while we're still here and long after we've left. That's a life of impact, and that's something that resonates with most people, from the billionaire executive of a *Fortune* 500 company to the high school graduate still trying to figure out who he wants to be when he grows up. Maybe it's resonating with you right now.

Earlier in this book, I challenged you to write your own epitaph. That is, look far into the future and imagine your own funeral. I know it seems weird. Even most people in their eighties haven't given this any thought. But from an impact perspective of the totality of your life, think about it! Who is there? Who is mourning your loss? Who and what have you left behind? What void has your passing left in your community or in the world as a whole? Who gives the eulogy? What does this person say about you? What's written on your tombstone?

It is a great irony that who we are in life becomes clearest only after we're dead. Have you ever noticed that some of the greatest writers, artists, and composers in history received barely any recognition at all in their own lifetime? It was only after their death that they gained the notoriety they deserved in life. That's true for us as well. Most of us will never know the impact we've had on the world this side of heaven. And, of course, we won't get the chance to sneak into our own funerals. So we have to imagine it. We have to project ourselves into the future and picture every detail of how we want to be remembered. Then we have to get about the difficult task of *living to become that person* in the time we have left. What we do with the time we have builds our legacy—one piece, one day, at a time.

I have tried to give you many strategies for creating a life of impact while growing and defending your financial pie. From facing your fears and pushing past limitations to the nuts and bolts of real estate and stock market investing, we've run the gamut on how to get from where you are right now to where you want go.

But I've saved the most important lesson for last.

START-STOP-MORE-LESS

Of all the different lessons I've learned over the years, of the myriad strategies and wealth-building tools I've used every day for more than three decades, the most powerful lesson is probably the simplest. In fact, it's so simple, even my eight-year-old son could master it after one conversation. And no, it's not about pies or taxes or mutual funds. It's about *change*. You see, I've learned that the key to getting more out of life is ... (drumroll) ... to do something different. As the old saying goes, "If you always do what you've always done, you'll always get what you've always gotten." What you've always done has brought you to where you are. To get where you want to go, however, you've got to make a change.

Now, you've probably heard that before. But I like to take the call to "make a change" a little further. Throughout my life, I've found that there are only four decisions we can make that will spark a life-altering change in our lives. I call it the *Start-Stop-More-Less Principle*. Put simply, the only four choices that really move the needle in our lives are the decisions to

1. *Start* something you've never done.
2. *Stop* something that's not working.
3. *Do more* of something that is taking you closer to where you want to go.
4. *Do less* of something that isn't getting you there (or isn't getting you there efficiently).

Everything you have now and ever will have comes from either *starting* something, *stopping* something, *doing more* of something, or *doing less* of something.

For example, if you've been an employee your entire life and know in your gut you could double your income within a year by leaving your "safe" job and starting your own business, you clearly have something to *start*: a new business. If you are in an abusive relationship that's slowly wearing you down and destroying your hope and self-image, you know what you need to *stop*: your relationship. If having lunch with a mentor once a month is having a big impact on your growth, find more mentors and *do more* lunches. If playing video games for three hours every night is getting in the way of the progress you want to make, *do less* of it. Start, stop, more, less. This isn't rocket science, is it? As my Aunt Ruby used to say, "Common sense is not as common as it used to be."

The problem is, we all fall into ruts. We become creatures of habit, even if those habits leave our lives stuck in neutral. If we want to move forward, then we have to change gears. And it doesn't have to be massive change overnight. It can be inch by inch. Hey, an inch of progress is *still* progress!

In chapter 1, I talked about *The 1 Percent Rule*. The whole idea around The 1 Percent Rule is making tiny, incremental changes every day. If you do this faithfully every day, you should become twice as productive in that area after only seventy-two days, per the Rule of 72. Keep going, and you'll double the productivity again after another seventy-two days. Then again. Then again. And, as you become more successful in *one* area of your life, you'll find that you're becoming more successful in *every* area of your life. That's because success breeds success. As you improve one thing, everything else seems to get better. It's the "rising tide effect," which states that a rising tide raises all ships. Put simply, if you pump more success into your life, even in just one area, that success is going to raise the bar for *every* part of your life.

Let me demonstrate the power of the Start-Stop-More-Less Principle, The 1 Percent Rule, and the rising tide effect all working together by telling you about my friend, whom we'll call Tom. When I met Tom, he had only a high school education, was in his early thirties and married, and already had five little kids. His family had recently lost the single-wide trailer they lived in to repossession, and they'd just moved into an old, run-down, dirty little house that barely fit all seven of them. He was working in IT at the absolute bottom rung of the professional ladder, making about $28,000 a year, and Tom's wife homeschooled the kids. They weren't getting any help from their parents and were barely scraping by.

I liked Tom, I saw a lot of potential in him, but that potential was buried. Deep. The stress and poverty hadn't been kind to him and his wife, and you could tell just from looking at them that they'd basically given up. They had settled into the notion that *this* was all they'd ever have, and it sent them both into a mild depression. They'd both gained a lot of weight, they were having some health problems, and the light was fading behind their eyes. They needed help.

I approached Tom one afternoon and, in my characteristic brash-ness, I said, "Tom, let me ask you a question. Are you interested in making some improvements in your life to get a better result or are you happy where you are right now?"

"We're barely getting by," he said. "I'd actually love some help, especially from someone who's doing as well as you are."

I took a few minutes to explain the Start-Stop-More-Less Principle and The 1 Percent Rule. I showed him how he could change his life in a very short time if he simply committed to making small changes every day, set goals, and moved step by step away from where he was right then and toward where he wanted to go.

"Okay, now let me ask you another question. Are you the kind of guy who can take some pretty blunt advice, even if it feels like criti-cism, if it's for your own good?"

"Totally. I know what I'm doing isn't working. Let me have it."

"Then here's your first small 1 percent change. By this time tomorrow, do you think you can *not* look like a caveman? You have the worst unibrow I've ever seen!"

He had a mixture of shock and laughter on his face as he replied, "Oh my gosh! Is it really that bad?"

"Yes. It's all anyone can think about when they look at you."

And that's how Tom's journey to success started: by shaving his unibrow. That's about as "1 percent" as you can get!

Once that was taken care of, I told Tom to iron his clothes. "Every time I see you, it looks like you pulled your shirt out of a wad of laundry on the floor."

"That's funny," he said. "I actually keep my clothes in a pile in the corner of my bedroom. I guess I need to start ironing and hanging them up." Again, we identified another 1 percent change that kept him moving in the right direction.

Once we'd targeted and addressed the appearance-related issues, we moved on to his professional situation. I asked him what he made, and he said it was around $28,000. I said, "Okay, what does your boss make?" He guessed it was around $80,000, and so I asked, "What skills do you need to learn to be able to do the job he does?" That gave us our next set of 1 percent tasks. A year or two later, Tom had mastered his boss's job, gotten several promotions, and had worked his way up to $80,000 himself.

Then, we repeated the process that got him to that point. I asked him what his *new* boss made, and he guessed it was around $120,000. So, we identified the tasks that he needed to learn to get to that level and, again, he mastered them pretty quickly. However, he had gone as far up the ladder as he could go at the company (unless his executive leader quit). The old Tom would have seen this as an insurmountable limitation, but that guy was long gone, replaced by a new, intelligent, professional, creative problem-solver. This new Tom saw his valuable skill set as an asset and pitched a risky offer to his bosses: What if he quit his full-time job with them and became a consultant? That way, the company wouldn't have to pay him benefits, he could charge a monthly consulting fee (which came out of a different budget than regular payroll), and they could terminate the consulting relationship if he wasn't adding more value than he cost. They agreed, and he took the bold step of leaving the "safety" of a full-time job for the adventure of working for himself, trusting that he brought enough value in his field to support his huge family, which by then had grown to *seven* children. This is something the Tom of two or three years ago never would have considered, but it was the natural next step for him now. He'd progressed so far that quitting his job and starting his own consulting business was just a 1 percent change!

Five years after I first met Tom, he had gone from a depressed, underpaid, overstressed, entry-level IT guy to a highly respected and sought-after technology consultant making $25,000 a month. His annual income had gone from $28,000 to $300,000! That's more than a 1,000 percent income change in just a few years! It didn't happen overnight, but it certainly wasn't all that difficult. It just took a little time, a little focus, and a commitment to make a 1 percent change every day. He had to *start* ironing his clothes, setting goals, and improving his skill set. He had to *stop* living with a poor-me, "little man can't get ahead" attitude. He had to *stop* being a victim and *start* looking solely to himself for change. He did *more* job training, networking, reading, and audiobooks. He spent *less* time on video games and stopped hiding from his bosses.

As he went through this process, a funny thing happened in the other areas of his life. He started taking night classes and graduated from college. He and his wife both lost a tremendous amount of weight. Their marriage was reinvigorated. They developed deeper connections with friends and took advantage of new service opportunities through their church. His wife also had a remarkable turnaround of her own. As the homeschooling mother of seven, she obviously loved children. She had also always greatly respected and appreciated the involvement of her doula throughout her pregnancies and the births of her kids. The success Tom was pumping into their lives was contagious, and his wife began studying to become a doula herself. She helped with four babies her first year, then eight, then sixteen, and up to forty by the time Tom launched his consulting business. She was making $50,000 as a doula on top of his huge consulting income. Every single part of this family's life changed radically over the course of just five years—because they embraced the power of change. They believed they could, and they made it happen. One day, 1 percent at a time.

"WHAT IF I FAIL?"

You may have noticed throughout this journey with me that I dream, and I dream *big*. I'm not ashamed to admit that I'm a pretty confident guy who is aware that everything in life can change in the blink of an eye, and I am grateful for all I have. So, when I tell people like Tom, "You can become a millionaire," I mean it. It's really not that hard; it's been done millions of times. *Can* anybody do it? Yes. *Will* everybody do it? Absolutely not. But 99 percent of the time that's not because there isn't an *opportunity* for success. It's because the individual just won't do what it takes. Why?

In chapter 5, I unpacked many of the "success blockers" that stand between where you are right now and where you want to go. I talked at length in that chapter about fear, but as we near the end of this book, I want to bring it back around one last time. Specifically, I want to call out the fear of failure—perhaps the greatest pie-stealing thief of all.

The fear of failure will steal your pie faster than almost anything else. And I'm not just talking about your financial pie. When we allow fear to drive our decisions or, just as bad, paralyze us from making *any* decisions, we put *everything* at risk—our financial success, relationships, career, health, and any other "pie" we're trying to protect. In an effort to "play it safe," we're practically guaranteeing that we'll never reach our goals or grow beyond where we are right now. After all, how can we grow our pie when we're always shrinking back from opportunities? You may hate hearing this, but the risks required to grow in any area are usually the very things you're scared to do!

Trust me, I get it. I don't have some superhuman power over fear. For years, I was literally scared of saying *my own name* out loud! The thought of stuttering through one more round of introductions to a classroom full of potential bullies at a new school was overwhelming at times. I went home crying a lot . . . but I went back the next day. I had to. When you're a kid, you go to school whether your classmates are mean or not. You don't have a choice. But when you grow up, you *do* have choices. You can choose to hide yourself away, avoid confrontation, and back away from scary things. You can choose a small, "safe" little life because it's easy. But something tells me that's not what you want to do. After all, you wouldn't have read this entire book if you are the type of person who's willing to settle for what's "easy." My guess is you're the kind of person who's willing to shoot for the moon.

Shooting for the Moon

I was two years old when Apollo 11 landed on the moon. My family, along with the rest of the world, watched on black-and-white televisions as man left the Earth. When you're that age, you have a childlike wonder about the world. Anything seems possible—even something as crazy as stepping onto alien soil somewhere else in space. It wasn't until I got older that I really understood how *impossible* that first lunar mission really was. Who were these people who looked up, saw a dime-sized moon in the night sky, and said, "Yeah, we can fly a plane there"? No wonder doubters and conspiracy theorists persist today, more than fifty years later. Can you even imagine sitting in the cockpit of a rocket built by the lowest bidder and being controlled by technology less powerful than a current iPhone? Those who are too scared to dream big often can't accept the reality of the dreams others bring to life.

As a child, seeing the video of men walking on the moon was the most impressive thing I'd ever seen. As a man, I think what's even *more* impressive is the courage it took to take on such an overwhelming goal. When John F. Kennedy kicked off the race to the moon with a powerful speech seven years earlier, he made two promises: first, we would do it before the end of that decade, and second, it would be very, very hard. He said,

> We choose to go to the Moon in this decade and do the other things, not because they are easy, but because they are hard, because that goal will serve to organize and measure the best of our energies and skills, because that challenge is one that we are willing to accept, one we are unwilling to postpone, and one which we intend to win.[18]

Kennedy refused to allow Americans—from the scientists and engineers at NASA to the everyday businesspeople and homemakers across the country—to give in to the fear of failure. Failure was, in everyone's mind, simply not an option. As a result, just ten years after that speech, we'd landed on the moon six separate times. The impossible became so mundane, in fact, that we haven't been back since 1972. But now we know we *can* go back . . . anytime we want to.

Failure Is Not an Option

I said earlier that I do not allow my children to use the phrase, "I can't." Instead, I've taught them to say, "I presently struggle with..." The difference is huge, and it reveals something important about me: I don't really believe in failure. Or maybe, like Kennedy and the moon landing, I don't believe in failure as an option. I can't. As soon as I accept failure as an option, I'm willingly and willfully backing away from opportunity—and that is something I choose not to do.

Instead, I challenge you to *reject failure* and *accept setbacks*. I'm not crazy, and I don't have a Midas touch. Despite my best efforts, I haven't turned every opportunity into gold. I have fallen short on goals and completely missed others. But does that mean I've failed? Does that make me a failure? Absolutely not. Never. No way, no how.

Here's the deal: you will absolutely, positively have setbacks as you work toward your goals. You'll fall short, you'll make mistakes, other people will let you down, or you'll be taken by surprise by circumstances beyond your control. Maybe, like someone I know, you'll open a restaurant a month before a global pandemic shuts everything down for fifteen months. Please hear me on this: these are not failures; these are setbacks.

I don't see failure as circumstantial; I see it as a condition. It's very personal. In my mind, failure isn't something you *do*, it's something you *are*. That's why I rarely use the word—because I refuse to see myself as a failure. A setback, however, is a temporary situation. It just means you were actively going somewhere and got slightly delayed or sidetracked. It doesn't mean you failed, and it doesn't mean you'll *never* get where you were going. It's a delay. That's all. A setback means you *were* making progress, you got knocked down or pushed back a little bit, and then you got back up and kept making progress. The key thing to remember is that a setback is simply something that happens to you while you're progressing to where you want to be.

With that view, the only thing I'd actually consider a failure is allowing fear to stop you from even trying. In chapter 2, I quoted the great Earl Nightingale, who defined success as "the progressive realization of a worthy ideal (or goal)." That is, you're a success as long as you're moving toward a goal—even if you haven't reached it yet. Success comes the moment you take that first, big, scary step away from where you are and toward where you want to be. Every step after that only makes you *more* successful . . . even if it's a step backward. As long as you're moving, you're winning. But, if you refuse to work toward a goal—whether it's due to fear, laziness, self-pity, doubt, or any of a million other things—you are guaranteed to fail. Your fairy godmother isn't going to magically appear, pick you up, and deliver you safely to a successful future. You've got to take the steps yourself. It's up to you. Choosing to stay put is choosing to fail. Anything else, any step forward toward where you want to go starts a success journey—one in which you don't *become* a success but one in which you *are* a success.

Once you're moving, then, failure is truly not an option. Because you're *already* a success.

THE PIE OF LIFE

Early in this book, I said you could imagine any part of your life as a pie that's divided up into slices that you have to defend. Since then, we've focused exclusively on the financial pie. That's because money is something I'm pretty qualified to talk about and because money is an area that most people—especially people just starting out in life—tend to have the most questions about. It's also an area that many people screw up . . . big time. As I've shared in this book, there have been times in my life when my family has struggled financially, and there have been times when money has given me experiences and opportunities I once never could have imagined. I have earned millions, lost millions, made millions again, and been everywhere in between. Through everything, I've learned that, while money won't solve your problems, having a little money in the bank is a lot better than being broke. And having a *lot* of money in the bank gives you indescribable freedom. Freedom from a job you may hate. Freedom to live wherever you want. Freedom to travel. Freedom to experience life in a rich, new way.

Money is a powerful tool but a very unfulfilling master. Ultimately, it's the nonfinancial things in life that give you the most satisfaction. But having money to put kids, grandkids, and total strangers through college or to help single mothers in need is pretty awesome. Having some nice things along the way is also fun—as long as you know they are simply *things* and you continue to work on who you are as a person.

But I want to be crystal clear here as we reach the end of this book. At the end of the day, money is just money. It's not the end-all, be-all of a fulfilling, "rich" life. It's just *one part*. It's just one of many pies that we're called to grow and manage. It's not even the most important pie. The most important pie we have to grow, manage, and defend is the Pie of Life, which is divided into five slices I call the *Five Fs*: faith, family, fitness, finances, and friends. Keeping these five areas growing and well maintained is, I believe, the secret to a healthy, happy, well-rounded life. Let's break them down.

Slice #1: Faith

The first slice in the Pie of Life is *faith*. As a Christian, my faith is extremely important to me. I was blessed with Christian parents and a godly home, and that upbringing and those beliefs have been fundamental in forming the man I've become and the life I've lived. However, when I talk about faith in the Pie of Life, I'm not specifically talking about religious or spiritual faith; I mean faith in the general sense. Simply put, *what do you believe* and *what do you believe in*? Faith covers the gamut of beliefs. You may believe in freedom, democracy, and capitalism. You may believe in taking care of the environment. You may believe in the power of technology to improve the lives of people around the world. And, yes, you may also hold core spiritual beliefs. My point here is that faith is a much bigger part of the pie than simply whether you believe in God.

Your beliefs drive your decisions, so it's a good idea to pay attention to what you believe in. Don't take these things for granted. Instead, question them and challenge them. For example, if you get home from work every night and throw back three beers before bed, you could ask yourself, "Do I believe drinking this much is making me a better, more productive person?" If you sit in front of the television for five hours a night, you could ask, "Do I believe the time I'm spending watching TV is taking me closer to or further from my goals?" If you're consumed with making more and more money at the expense of your relationships, you could ask, "Do I believe more money will truly fill this emptiness I feel?" Everyone believes in something, and those beliefs are reflected in the choices we make. If you can't figure out why you aren't further along in reaching your goals, I challenge you to examine how your beliefs—your *faith*—is affecting your journey.

Slice #2: Family

The second slice is *family*. When I say family, what I really mean is, *who are the people you are "doing life with" on a daily basis?* This includes not only your spouse, children, parents, and siblings but also your closest friends. These are the people who go back ten, twenty, or fifty years, the ones you could call in the middle of the night and know they'd jump out of bed, get in the car, and race to help you no matter what. Most of us have no idea how much we are shaped by the people in our inner circles. These precious individuals are always top of mind; they're the ones we are working to provide a better life for, the ones we're striving to serve and protect, and the ones we know are there to serve and protect us. As Proverbs says, "A friend loves at all times, and a brother is born for a time of adversity" (17:17). Put another way, your family are the people who've got your back—always.

These kinds of bonds are priceless, and they need constant care and maintenance. Never, *never* neglect your family in pursuit of money. Sure, there will be nights when you have to work late, and there will be business trips or meetings that conflict with kids' soccer games. That's just life. But if your family *expects* you to let them down, you've got a much bigger problem than the size of your next paycheck. No amount of money is worth being truly alone in the world, and no amount can buy you one more minute of time to spend with your loved ones. Be sure you're protecting your family pie.

Slice #3: Fitness

The third slice is *fitness*, and by that I mean your health. Most people can have any level of health and fitness they want. Why, then, are obesity, depression, and sickness so prevalent here in the wealthiest country on earth? I believe it's because we aren't taking our health seriously enough. Our bodies are incredible machines, but they require quality fuel and routine maintenance. We can take the easy road with a fast-food diet and zero exercise for a while, but it'll catch up to us in the long run. Sometime—usually in your forties— things start to change. You get tired more easily. You get sick more often. Your joints hurt. Your belt buckle gets lost under a belly that appeared overnight. A "Take the Stairs" sign on a broken elevator becomes a terrifying sight.

We're each assigned one body when we enter the world, and we've got to make that body last. The more you take care of it, the more it'll take care of you, and the longer you'll be around to live, laugh, love, and build a legacy that can change your family, your community, and maybe even the world.

Slice #4: Finances

The fourth slice of the Pie of Life is *finances*. I've obviously said a lot about this subject throughout this book, so there's no point trying to rehash everything here. I will add, however, that the point of building wealth is not just to have fancy cars and big houses. I want you to have fun with money, but that should never be *all* we do with the wealth we've created. Money is a responsibility, and a *lot* of money is a *lot* of responsibility. Manage it well by finding ways to help others and improve the lives of people outside your immediate family. Like I said at the start of this chapter, think about what kind of impact you want to make on the world, then live (and give) to be that person.

Slice #5: Friends

The fifth and final slice of the Pie of Life is *friends*. As the great motivational speaker and sales trainer Jim Rohn used to say, "You are the average of the five people you spend the most time with." If you aren't making any headway toward your goals, you might need to take a good, hard look at the people you're hanging out with. Are they lifting you up or are they pulling you down? Are they feeding your growth? Are they pushing you forward? Are they encouragers, supporters, fans, and cheerleaders? Are they challenging you? Are they calling you out when you do something stupid?

Who we are and what we do is largely a matter of input and output. What we take in from the sources in our lives—what we read, watch, and listen to *and* who we spend time with—feeds into the man or woman we're becoming. It would be extremely unusual for a tight friend group of five buddies to include two million-aires, two minimum-wage earners, and one guy with an average income. It's much more likely that all five would have incomes within 20 percent of each other. That's why I think it's important for us to continually add people into our lives as our financial situation changes. I'd never suggest "cutting loose" your old high school and college friends just because they are in a different financial position from you, but I *am* suggesting that you become intentional about also finding friends who can understand and empathize with what your life looks like as you build wealth. Even millionaires need someone to talk to about the challenges that come with wealth. If I tried to talk about the trouble I'm having buying a Topgolf location with one of my friends from high school who chose a different path, though, they'd just roll their eyes and give me the "poor little rich boy" treatment. That's no good for anyone. We'd both come away from that discussion irritated.

Your parents were right: who you hang out with *does* have an influence on you. So make sure you've got the right influences at the right time as you work toward your goals.

Keep the Pie Round

Faith, family, fitness, finances, and friends. That's a healthy, well-rounded Pie of Life. When we give each area equal treatment, we keep the pie nice and round. When we focus too much on any one area at the expense of the others, though . . . well, that's when we end up with a weird, misshapen mess of a pie. Do not let your pursuit of one *F* destroy the other four. All five are important, and no single one is *the* thing that will give your life meaning and purpose. Your life is and should remain a balance of all five areas.

Often, when we're young, we are willing to give up our faith, family, fitness, and friends in the pursuit of finances. We stop going to church, give up our prayer time, miss dinners with the family, stop working out, shove fast food down our throats between business meetings, and lose track of lifelong friends all so we can devote more time and attention to our careers. We act like we have all the time in the world to make up for what we're giving up in the name of money. But then we look up one day and we're old. You could be a seventy-year-old billionaire, but what's the point if your family hates you, you have no friends, you're terminally ill, and you have no faith to cling to? Does that sound like winning to you—rich, sick, and all alone? At that point, you'll spend all your money just to get back what you gave up. But by then it's usually too late.

Don't get to that point. Instead, use the Five Fs as a dashboard for life. Keep them in front of you all the time. Have regular check-ins when you run through each one, asking yourself, *How am I doing with faith? Is my family in good shape? How's my fitness? Are my finances where they need to be? Are my friends sparking growth in me?* If one or more of these is shrinking away, redirect time from the others to bring it back to life. If one is twice the size of the others, cut it down and invest that time and energy into the other four. You'll never have perfect balance in every area of life, but it's still a goal worth striving toward. Just staying mindful of all five areas helps ensure we're taking care of ourselves, keeping our priorities in check, and not outrunning the friends and family who are doing life alongside us.

PLAY THE LONG GAME

In all my years working with people at all levels of wealth, I've discovered one practically universal truth: most people *overestimate* what they can accomplish in the short term and almost always *underestimate* what they can accomplish over the long term. Mastery in any area of life—including finances—doesn't happen in the short term. It just doesn't. Yeah, you can have some huge wins that move the needle. I've had my fair share of once-in-a-lifetime opportunities that have set me up to win bigger and better than ever before. I've had days when the stars aligned, and I made a pile of quick cash on a real estate deal or stock transaction. Those are exciting days! But I've never had a single day, week, or month that I'd consider my "make or break" moment. Those are all just short-term wins. It's great when they happen, but I don't pin my long-term success on short-term victories. Instead, I play the long game.

Success in any area—faith, family, fitness, finances, and friendship—takes time. You can't go from a baby Christian to a world-class theologian after taking a six-week Bible class. You can't go from beer belly to six-pack abs after two workouts. And you won't go from broke to billionaire overnight. That's actually a good thing. Most people who have those "strike it rich" moments lose all their money within a year or two because they didn't take the time to learn how to manage that money wisely. It slips through their fingers almost as quickly as it appeared. Just research what happens to broke people within five years of winning the lottery. It's tragic. So, my goal with this book hasn't been to give you a shortcut to getting rich; rather, I've focused on giving you a road map for building wealth over the long haul.

I want you to win, and I want you to win *big*. I believe you can because I know from my personal experience and the experiences of hundreds of other millionaires and billionaires I've worked with that *anyone* can. But it takes time, focus, and a commitment to set and achieve huge goals. It won't be easy, and it won't be overnight, but you can do it if you can apply what we've discussed throughout this book by

- Pushing back on all the negative self-talk that tries to sabotage your efforts.
- Clearly identifying where you are right now and visualizing where you want to go.
- Bridging the vocation, education, time, and attitude gaps that are standing in your way.
- Being proactive in taking advantage of all the benefits and tax-favored retirement options available to you as either an employee or entrepreneur.
- Investing intelligently in real estate and/or marketable securities.

Most importantly, though, I want to challenge you to look for the opportunity behind every limitation. If you can do just that, if you can push past the limits and grab hold of the opportunities even *some* of the time, you'll experience a level of success most people only dream about.

You can have your pie . . . and eat it too.

Acknowledgments

Writing this book has been a lifelong dream come true, but it absolutely would not have been possible without the encouragement, direction, prayers, support, and occasional kick in the butt from the wonderful team who came together to help me bring this book to life. I'd like to say a special word of thanks to:

Allen Harris, my developmental editor, who tirelessly helped a first-time writer break through writer's block and kept me on a weekly track that helped get this lifetime goal completed. Allen, you're amazing and gifted at helping people not only find their voice but, helping them impact others by getting their message out.

Jonathan Merkh and Jen Gingerich, my publishing team at Forefront Books. Thank you for your encouragement, project management, and publishing expertise in taking this first-time author from manuscript to a real, honest-to-goodness book people can read and use to change their lives!

Dave Schroeder and my team at WTA Media. Thank you for connecting me with the right people to get this project off the ground and for all you've done to help promote it.

Jerry O'Neal, who helped organized the endless meetings, calls, and Zoom work sessions required to make this book happen.

James Kinard and friends at Useful Group, who have helped me build and create content for social media. I would be lost in social media without your help. It's great being able to track interactions and see how books can positively impact people's lives.

Chris Roslan from Roslan and Associates Public Relations. Thanks for making the PR world accessible to a first-time author. PR can be overwhelming, and your experience and the ways you have taught me messaging and impact have been very valuable.

Notes

1 U.S. Inflation Calculator: 1635–2021, Department of Labor Data, calculated July 9, 2021, https://www.google.com/search?q=1996+%241+adjusted+for+inflation&sxsrf=ALeKk02Dn45IQEqN6qkgf7reZNlnVbxLew%3A1625840690811&ei=MlzoYKX0MJOGtQb216HADA&oq=1996+%241+adjusted+for+inflation&gs_lcp=Cgdnd3Mtd2l6EAMyBggAEAgQHjIFCAAQhgM6BwgAEEcQsAM6CAgAEAgQBxAeSgQIQRgAULKnElicqhJgpK0SaAFwAngAgAFciAHpAZIBATOYAQCgAQGqAQdnd3Mtd2l6yAEIwAEB&sclient=gws-wiz&ved=0ahUKEwil1djGmNbxAhUTQ80KHfZrCMgQ4dUDCA4&uact=5.

2 William Shakespeare, *Measure for Measure*, Act I, Scene IV.

3 Brian Tracy, "The Value of a Long-Term Perspective," American Management Association, April 11, 2019, https://www.amanet.org/articles/the-value-of-a-long-term-perspective/#:~:text=Edward%20Banfield%20of%20Harvard%20University,course%20of%20their%20working%20lifetimes.

4 *The Complete Plays of George Bernard Shaw (1893-1921), 34 Complete and Unabridged Plays Including: Mrs. Warren's Profession, Caesar and Cleopatra, Man* (Oxford City, UK, 2012).

5 "Self-Employed and the U.S. Economy," National Association for the Self-Employed (NASE), https://www.nase.org/sf-docs/default-source/research-results/self-employed-and-the-u-s-economy--aug2012.pdf?sfvrsn=2%22.

6 Michael Hyatt, *Free to Focus: A Total Productivity System to Achieve More by Doing Less* (Grand Rapids, MI: Baker Books, 2019), 14.

7 Duncan Haughey, "A Brief History of SMART Goals," Project Smart, December 13, 2014, https://www.projectsmart.co.uk/brief-history-of-smart-goals.php.

8 Erin El Issa, "Nerdwallet's 2020 American Household Credit Card Debt Study,"

Nerdwallet, January 12, 2021, https://www.nerdwallet.com/blog/average-credit-card-debt-household/.

9 Anna Helhoski and Ryan Lane, "Student Loan Debt Statistics: 2021," NerdWallet.com, June 14, 2021, https://www.nerdwallet.com/article/loans/student-loans/student-loan-debt.

10 Charlene Rhinehart, "Peter Thiel's $5 Billion Roth IRA Secret Could Make You Rich," *The Motley Fool*, July 17, 2021, https://www.fool.com/investing/2021/07/17/peter-thiels-5-billion-roth-ira-secret-make-rich/.

11 Michael T. Nietzel, "What Does a Year of College Really Cost?," *Forbes*, October 26, 2020, https://www.forbes.com/sites/michaeltnietzel/2020/10/26/what-does-a-year-of-college-really-cost/?sh=1783125c7bad.

12 Peter Miller, "U.S. Home Prices Hit a Record High in 2020. Is Home Buying Still Affordable?," *The Mortgage Reports*, October 13, 2020, https://themortgagereports.com/70539/record-high-prices-record-low-mortgage-rates-during-covid.

13 Miller, "U.S. Home Prices Hit a Record High."

14 Richard Fry, "Millennials Overtake Baby Boomers as America's Largest Generation," Pew Research Center, April 28, 2020, https://www.pewresearch.org/fact-tank/2020/04/28/millennials-overtake-baby-boomers-as-americas-largest-generation/.

15 Fry, "Millennials Overtake Baby Boomers."

16 Fry, "Millennials Overtake Baby Boomers."

17 Matthew DeBord, "Here's How Tesla Went from Elon Musk's Infamous $420 Tweet to Being Worth Almost $500 per Share," *Business Insider*, January 11, 2020, https://www.businessinsider.com/elon-musk-420-tweet-timeline-analysis-through-2020-2020-1.

18 John F. Kennedy, "John F. Kennedy Moon Speech—Rice Stadium," September 12, 1962, https://er.jsc.nasa.gov/seh/ricetalk.htm.